FORTUNE-TELLING WITH NUMBERS

Shows how numbers can help you understand your character and talents and enable you to know your own destiny.

FORTUNE-TELLING WITH NUMBERS

Knowing Yourself and Your Fate Through Numerology

by

RODNEY DAVIES

THE AQUARIAN PRESS
Wellingborough, Northamptonshire

First published July 1986
Second Impression December 1986

British Library Cataloguing in Publication Data

Davies, Rodney
Fortune telling with numbers.
1. Fortune-telling with numbers
I. Title
133.3'354   BF1891.N8

ISBN 0-85030-486-5

The Aquarian Press is part of the Thorsons Publishing Group

Printed and bound in Great Britain

CONTENTS

PART ONE:
NUMBERS AND THE PRESENT

1

YOUR IMPORTANT NUMBERS

This book shows you how to understand your character and your talents through numbers, and how numbers can reveal the general pattern of your life, so enabling you to know your destiny. It also tells you how to find your lucky days and dates, and how to use numbers to improve your fortune.

The use of numbers in this way constitutes numerology, which is an ancient divinatory art dating back at least as far as the sixth century BC, when the Greek mathematician and philosopher Pythagoras taught at his school at Croton, in Italy, that everything is number.

In a very real sense Pythagoras was right, because number is an integral part of the natural world. Each of us, for example, is formed from a genetically predetermined number of bodily parts – one heart, two eyes, ten fingers, and so on – which make us the beings we are, and every scientist knows that counting is as important to the classifier as the examination of shape, colour and size. Indeed, the chemical elements that are the building blocks of life differ from one another only because their atoms are made up of different numbers of protons, neutrons and electrons.

Number imposes order on nature and in so doing creates its beauty – think for a moment of the hexagonal ice crystals of snowflakes and the trefoil leaves of clover – because line, form and symmetry are the products of number. And it is because numbers comprise the essence of ourselves that they can be used as keys to our personality and our abilities and to our path through life.

The numbers that we are going to be concerned with are the nine single numbers running from 1 to 9. These, together with zero, constitute the bricks and mortar of numeration because every number, from 10 up, is expressed as combinations of them.

Where appropriate we shall reduce all numbers larger than 9 to a single number. This is done by adding the constituent numbers together. Take the number 301, for example, which is made of 3, 0 and 1. When these are added together they total 4:

$$3 + 0 + 1 = 4$$

For numbers whose constituents when first added give a double number, the addition must be continued until a single number is obtained. Consider 989, for example:

$$9 + 8 + 9 = 26$$

The product is 26. To get a single number the 2 and the 6 must be added together:

$$2 + 6 = 8$$

Of course, for larger numbers further additions may be necessary.

In numerology both the individual digits of a number (the 3, 0 and 1 of 301, and the 9, 8 and 9 of 989) and its single product are important, although zero, not being a number, has qualities only of space and not of character.

Your most important numbers are those of your birthdate. Taken individually, these represent the day, the month and the year of your birth.

The day number always falls somewhere between 1 and 31.

The month number depends on the placement of the month in the year. January is the first month, February the second month, and so on, right through to December, which is the twelfth month. Each month is numbered accordingly.

The year of birth may be in the late 1800s for someone who is very old, but for most people the birth year will be 1900 and something.

For example, consider the birthdate 7 April 1963. Because April is the fourth month of the year this date is expressed numerically as 7-4-1963.

The *day number* is always placed first, the *month number* second and the *year* last. This is because the day number is most personal to you, while the year is least personal. Many millions of people were born throughout the world in 1963, for instance. About a twelfth of them were born in the month of April, and of these about a thirtieth were born on the 7th.

In Britain it is usual to write the above date as 7-4-1963, but in

America it is the practice to put the month number first, followed by the day number and then the year. Thus in America 7 April 1963 is written 4-7-1963. This would be as confusing to a Briton, who would think it meant 4 July 1963, as the Briton's 7-4-1963 would be to an American, who would read it as the same date, 4 July 1963.

Your birthdate will give a similar sequence of numbers, which together represent your character and your talents, just as the planets and their placement in the zodiac do on your day of birth. In fact, as we shall shortly discover, the link between numerology and astrology is close.

When the numbers of your birthdate are added together and the product reduced to a single number, the result is the *birth* or *destiny number*. This number symbolizes the course and general tenor of your life, or your destiny.

This is how our example birthdate adds up:

$$7 + 4 + 1 + 9 + 6 + 3 = 30$$
$$3 + 0 = 3$$

The birth or destiny number of someone born on 7 April 1963 is therefore 3. You can calculate your birth number in the same way. This is also your *lucky number* because it rules those periods of your life which are luckiest for you. These periods are dealt with later.

The other numbers which are personally important to you are the ones that can be obtained from your name. There are three of these: the *vowel number*, the *consonant number* and the *name number* itself. They are calculated using the table below, which gives the number equivalents of the letters of the alphabet:

1	2	3	4	5	6	7	8	9
A	B	C	D	E	F	G	H	I
J	K	L	M	N	O	P	Q	R
S	T	U	V	W	X	Y	Z	

The five vowels are *a*, *e*, *i*, *o*, and *u*, and these have the values 1, 5, 9, 6 and 3 respectively. The vowel number of a name is determined by adding together the values of its vowels. Let us take the name John Smith by way of example, which has two vowels, *o* and *i*.

JOHN SMITH
6   +   9   = 15 = 6

The vowel number of John Smith's name is therefore 6.

The consonant number is obtained in an identical way, by adding together the number values of the name's consonants:

$$\text{JOHN SMITH}$$
$$1 \quad 8\ 5\ 14 \quad 2\ 8 = 29 = 11 = 2$$

The consonant number of John Smith's name is 2. (Note that here we have had to go one stage further in our additions, since 11 is a two-digit number.)

Likewise, the name number is obtained by adding together all the letter values and by reducing the product to a single number:

$$\text{JOHN SMITH}$$
$$16\ 8\ 5 \quad 1\ 4\ 9\ 2\ 8 = 44 = 8$$

More simply, the name number can be determined by adding together the vowel number and the consonant number:

$$6 + 2 = 8$$

The three numbers which can be obtained from the name John Smith are therefore 6, 2 and 8.

But what if John Smith has a middle name, such as Arthur? Should all three names be used to determine the vowel number, the consonant number and the name number? The answer is No – unless Mr Smith thinks of himself as and calls himself John Arthur Smith. Numerologists are agreed that, in general, the only names that should be considered numerologically are the family name or surname and the commonly used Christian or first name, or its contraction, or the pet name.

So while Mr Smith's full name is John Arthur Smith, he is for numerological purposes John Smith – or Arthur Smith if he uses the name Arthur in preference to John. Of course, if he has taken to using the name Arthur but has contracted it to Art, he must be considered as Art Smith.

In a similar way, pet names must be evaluated if they are used by the people concerned, just as Mo must be for Maureen, Bill for William, Jack for John and Sandy for Sandra if Mo, Bill, Jack and Sandy call themselves by these names.

Because our name reflects our sense of self, it is hardly surprising that we may change it as we grow and mature. Thus someone named Elizabeth might prefer to be known as Betty when she's a schoolgirl, as Liz when she's a young woman and as Elizabeth only when she's married and settled down.

In contrast to the birthdate numbers, which represent our basic or inherited character, the name numbers represent our character as it is moulded by our environment.

The vowel number symbolizes our exposed or conscious self. In Freudian terms it represents our *ego*.

The consonant number symbolizes our hidden or unconscious self. In Freudian terms it therefore represents our *id*.

Together, the vowel number and the consonant number combine to give the name number, which in turn represents our total personality. Thus the name is the measure of the man.

As the vowel number can be matched with any one of the nine possible consonant numbers, this means that although there are only nine ego personalities and nine id personalities, there are eighty-one total personalities ($9 \times 9 = 81$).

A balanced personality has an ego and an id which interact harmoniously with each other, while an unbalanced personality does not. Such harmony or disharmony is revealed by the degree of compatibility or incompatibility between the vowel and the consonant numbers. Incompatible numbers point to personality problems of one sort or another.

There are five *odd* single numbers – 1, 3, 5, 7 and 9 – and four *even* single numbers – 2, 4, 6 and 8. In general, odd and even numbers are incompatible, thus their presence together usually indicates inner tensions and difficulties.

The odd numbers represent the qualities of hardness, action, extroversion, leadership, aggression, motivation, domination and ambition – in other words, those qualities traditionally linked with the male – while the even numbers symbolize female softness, stillness, passiveness, introversion, submission and unambition. More widely, odd numbers stand for active qualities – heat, light, strength, weight, speed, etc. – and even numbers for inactive qualities – cold, darkness, weakness, lightness, slowness, and so on.

Equally, the odds are linked with the good forces of the world, with honesty, openness, truth, etc., and thus ultimately with God Himself, while the evens are the numbers of the Left-Hand Path, of dishonesty, concealment, untruth, etc., and hence of the Devil. Yet it would be wrong to pursue this too far and to equate the male and the active only with good and the female and inactive only with evil, for this is simply not true. The universe is built of opposites and these have equal importance in its construction, thus they are in themselves neither good nor bad. In this respect we should remember that philosophers and mystics have long said that in terms of achieving the best from life, one should always seek out a Middle Way, the Golden Mean.

2

NUMBERS AND YOU

There exists, as the last chapter mentioned, a close connection between numerology and astrology. This is hardly surprising in view of the fact that everything in the universe has a numerical base. Indeed, we can even go so far as to say that if the planets circling the Sun control our destiny, then their power derives from number. And this means that because the secret of life and of those forces acting on living things lies with numbers, we can, through a study of numbers, understand mysteries that have long seemed impenetrable.

Each planet has a certain influence over an individual's person and life. When one planet's influence is strong the individual shows signs of it, both in looks and character and in life pattern. This is in accordance with the central dictum of astrology – as above, so below. Of course, it is impossible for anyone to be wholly under the influence of one planet. We are all planetary mixtures, and have variable life patterns to match.

The ancient astrologers knew of only five planets – Mercury, Venus, Mars, Jupiter and Saturn – and the Sun and the Moon. But because the latter were also called planets, the ancients spoke of 'the seven planets' and gave due reverence to the number 7. But more importantly, as far as we are concerned, they identified each of the nine single numbers with one of the seven planets, thus linking each number with distinct planetary characteristics and powers. The list below gives these traditional number/planet matchings:

> 1 and 4 : THE SUN
> 2 and 7 : THE MOON
> 3 : JUPITER
> 5 : MERCURY

6 : VENUS
8 : SATURN
9 : MARS

Two numbers, 1 and 4, are associated with the Sun, and two, 2 and 7, with the Moon. This 'doubling up' with respect to two of the planets is necessary because there are nine single numbers but only seven planets. However, since the discovery of the 'new' planets Uranus, Neptune and Pluto, some numerologists have ascribed 4 to Uranus and 7 to Neptune, while Pluto has been linked with both 8 and 9. But because these associations are both uncomfortable and disputed they will, for the purposes of this book, be ignored.

Just as the nine single numbers represent natural order, so zero – 0 – stands for space and emptiness, the original Chaos from which matter arose. Such formlessness was the starting point of creation in most mythologies. In the Greek Pelasgian creation myth, for example, the goddess Eurynome ('wide wandering') rises naked from Chaos, and, finding nothing on which to rest her feet, separates the sea from the sky and dances upon the waves.

The nothingness which preceded the creation was called Nirgun Brahman, or Brahma's Night, by the Hindus. Creation or the start of Brahma's Day was brought about by the explosive creative principle named Savitar, the Sun god, who manifested in a manner resembling the Big Bang of modern astronomy, suddenly flooding the universe with light and heat.

In Genesis, Chapter 1, God says on the fourth day of creation, 'Let there be lights in the firmament to divide the day from the night.' He then made 'the greater light' – that is, the Sun – 'to rule the day, and the lesser light' – the Moon – 'to rule the night.' This Biblical story partly explains why the Sun, the first celestial body to be created on the fourth day, is linked with numbers 1 and 4, and why the Moon, the second celestial body to be created, is linked with 2. The Moon is also associated with 7 because each stage of its cycle takes seven days.

The five remaining numbers, viz. 3, 5, 6, 8 and 9, each became associated with one of the five visible planets. How this came about and the effect that it had on the meanings of the numbers themselves is dealt with in detail on the following pages.

The Number 1

1 is an enigmatic number, despite its apparent simplicity. One of

anything may represent the least you can have, yet it is also the first step in gaining more of the same. Indeed, the notion of the first – 'the first step', 'first place', 'first in line' – is as much one of making the initial move as it is of being the winner. But while 'first away, first home' seems a persuasive argument, one should never forget Aesop's fable of the tortoise and the hare.

Because 1 is the first number, rising from zero just as Eurynome rose from Chaos, it stands for both new beginnings and for all that may follow. After all, every succeeding number is only an ever growing group of 1's: 2 is two 1's, 3 is three 1's, and so on *ad infinitum.*

As one of the two numbers linked specifically with the Sun, 1 is the number of the rising Sun (called Khepri by the Egyptians) which brings the new day. Yet because 1 comprises every other number, they, too, can be identified with different stages of the Sun's cycle. The sequence 1 to 9 is a solar sequence, endlessly repeated as 10 to 18, 19 to 27, 28 to 36, 37 to 45, 46 to 54, 55 to 63, 64 to 72, 73 to 81, 82 to 90, 91 to 99, etc.

2 represents the Sun at mid-morning, when it is still rising and when its heat is not too intense. 3 is the Sun at noon, the all-seeing Re of the Egyptians, at the height of its power and splendour. 4 is the Sun of mid-afternoon, sinking towards the western horizon, and 5 is the number of the setting Sun, Atum.

6, 7 and 8 are the numbers of the Sun in the underworld. 6 symbolizes the Sun's descent into the nether regions, 7 the Sun at its nadir, its deepest and most mysterious point, and 8 represents the Sun beginning its journey back to the world of men.

9 stands for the final stage of the Sun's journey, which is both an end and a beginning, for a 'new' and rejuvenated solar disc is about to appear in the sky. Indeed, if 1 is envisaged as symbolizing the half of the Sun above the horizon, 9 represents the half still below it.

The diagram at the top of the next page makes these number equivalents clear.

1 is the number of birth and of new life generally, of new starts and of confident moves forward, of climbing above difficulties, of aiming high, of breaking with the past, and of energy and enthusiasm. It is the number of youth, daring, single-mindedness, sexual awakening and adventure. It is also the number of the risen God, the deity who dies but who overcomes death to be born again, as did Tammuz, the vegetation god of the Babylonians, the

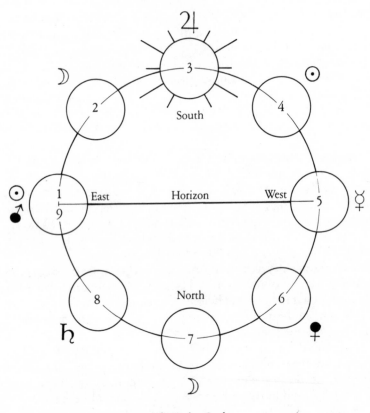

The Solar Cycle

Egyptian Osiris, who rose from the dead as Horus, and Jesus Christ, who 'rose from the dead and who ascended into heaven'.

1 is plentifully endowed with the qualities of the first: activity, motivation, leadership, pluck, ambition, direction and purpose, that is, with those qualities that are masculine and aggressive. But in keeping with the Sun's placement on the horizon, where it is just starting its climb into the sky, 1 is also the number of the child and of childish traits: naïvety, awkwardness, self-consciousness, selfishness, cruelty and gullibility. 1 thus symbolizes strength, vigour and immaturity.

If you were born on the 1st of any month, 1 is an important

influence in your life, as it is if you were born on the 10th or the 11th. Indeed, the 11th born are doubly influenced by 1. 1 traits are also found in those with birthdays on the 12th, 13th, 14th, 15th, 16th, 17th, 18th, 19th, 21st and 31st, although these are admixed with those represented by the other number. 1 is also important in the lives of those born in January, the first month, as well as those born in October (the tenth month), November (the eleventh month) and, although to a lesser extent, December (the twelfth month). Famous people with birthdays on the 1st include Louis Bleriot (1-7-1872), Jimmy Carter (1-10-1924), Olivia de Havilland (1-7-1916), Marilyn Monroe (1-6-1926), Joe Orton (1-1-1933), Lytton Strachey (1-3-1880) and Edgar Wallace (1-4-1895).

If 1 is strongly represented in your birthdate you are of average height or above and have a lean, athletic body. You carry yourself well, keeping your head up and your shoulders back. You have large, striking eyes, a lot of hair and a very good skin. Indeed, your whole appearance and demeanour suggest vibrancy and confidence, which is why heads turn when you enter the room. Because you love being the centre of attention you may behave childishly if you're ignored. If this doesn't bring results, you quickly return to those who know your worth. Your immaturity is often expressed by an over-eagerness for new and different things, by a readiness to support crank causes and by your tendency to sulk when you cannot get your own way. Yet your positive and enthusiastic nature is stimulating and attractive, gaining you many friends and admirers. Because you are by nature a leader and not a follower, you find it hard to take orders or even to work with others on an equal footing, for you like being the boss and directing operations. However, you are basically rather conservative, thus you never intentionally kick against the pricks. You also have a strong sense of loyalty and a love of fair play.

1 is the number of gold and of similar light, bright colours. In physical terms it represents health and fitness, fleetness of foot, blonde hair, skin that tans easily and attractive features. The direction of 1 is east, and travel to the east or residence in that part of the country is fortunate for those with 1 prominent in their birthdate. The luckiest period of the year for 1s is between 20 March and 20 April, when the Sun passes through Aries, where it is exalted, while the worst is between 24 September and 23 October, when the Sun is debilitated in Libra.

Should you possess a 1 vowel number, which is symbolic of your ego personality, you are blessed with an open, friendly and confident manner. Yet your nature is paradoxical because your confidence stems from a childish belief in your own superiority. Indeed, you are basically selfish, to the extent that you only give your friendship to those who accept your elevated ideas about yourself. You are, however, a good leader and organizer, and you are not afraid of making decisions or of taking responsibility. You hate work that is boring or repetitive, or that requires you to dirty your hands, which is why manual jobs are not for you. In fact, your love of being in the public eye means that work as an actor, entertainer or politician represents your employment ideal. If you are a woman you don't much like housework or looking after children. Money is important to you and you have quite expensive tastes: you like to dress well, live in elegant surroundings, and entertain in some style. You are probably not a smoker or a drinker. You dislike rudeness, and those that behave badly in your house never get invited back. You hate being on your own; thus you can only feel complete in the company of others. Your generosity and warmth make you popular and win you friends, although your friendship, as noted above, is not readily given. You are proud of your family and interested in its history.

An ego symbolized by 1, the number of the rising Sun, is ideally complemented by an id represented by 5, the number of the setting Sun. A 7 id is also a satisfactory match because it gives you an emotional depth that might otherwise be lacking. You are similarly well served by a 3 id, which not only realistically increases your self-confidence but matures and stabilizes you. But a 1 id or a 9 id cannot make your ego a good partner because their characters are too close to its own, especially inasmuch as they are selfish and immature. An id symbolized by an even number – 2, 4, 6 or 8 – is not generally favourable, with perhaps the exception of a 4 id, which can, 4 being the second solar number, provide sufficient strength and stability to balance you. Of the rest, a 6 id is better than a 2 id or an 8 id.

If 1 is your consonant number, representing your id or unconscious, you have a strong innate sense of your own self-worth and of the general rightness of your ideas. How this inner certainty manifests depends on your ego type, but you will always feel driven to put the world to rights; thus you have a tendency to tell others how they should behave. You have very high standards and you are contemptuous of the morally weak. Indeed, your 1 id is something of a taskmaster because it demands much from you: it won't let you settle for second-best in either your working life or your relationships and it constantly pressurizes you to improve yourself. In this respect, Excelsior is your watchword. Yet because 1 ids are the sunniest of all, you seldom get depressed and when you do, your black mood does not last for long. This helps you to recover quickly from set-backs and disappointments and prevents you from being self-pitying. Such an id also gives you stable and sustained emotions, thus when you give your heart you give it completely. Promiscuity is not your style, which means that if your ego decides to have a fling you will feel both guilty and ashamed. You enjoy being at home with your family and if you have to travel you will try to take your loved ones with you.

If your name number is 1 you adore sunny days, the open air and visits to forests and mountains. You are fascinated by old forts, castles and battle sites. You enjoy giving advice, helping others, bitter tastes, gold jewellery, thick clothes, your father's company, being with members of the armed forces, dogs and horses, and anything to do with royalty. Your lucky day of the week is Sunday; your lucky gemstones are the diamond, the amber, the sardonyx and the topaz; your lucky flowers are the cowslip, the heliotrope, the marigold and the sunflower; and your lucky colours are gold, orange, yellow and yellow-green.

The Number 2

2 is one of the two numbers linked with the Moon and it is called the number of the Positive Moon. In the solar cycle 2 represents the Sun at mid-morning, when it is well above the horizon but not yet too hot.

The Moon is identified with two numbers because it follows a continuously changing cycle, one consisting of a waxing or growth phase and the other of a waning or shrinkage phase. These two phases also naturally link the Moon with 2, as do the Moon's two horns which it displays when New. And because each stage of the Moon's cycle, from New Moon to First Quarter Moon, from First Quarter Moon to Full Moon, from Full Moon to Second Quarter Moon, and from Second Quarter Moon to Old Moon takes seven days, the number 7 is similarly associated with the Moon. Indeed, 7 is known as the number of the Negative Moon. Taken together, 2 represents the waxing Moon, its positive phase, and 7 the waning Moon, its negative phase.

The Moon is, without doubt, the most interesting of the heavenly bodies. It is large, easily observable and ever-changing.

It greatly impressed early man, who revered it above the Sun. And while we think of the Moon as having female characteristics, many ancient societies regarded the Moon as a male god. The Sumerians believed that the Moon, whom they called Nanna, was the father of both the Sun (or Utu) and Venus (or Inanna). And as late as the Middle Ages the Scandinavians thought that the Moon was a boy and the Sun a girl, who rode across the sky in chariots fleeing from pursuing wolves. The world would end, they said, when the wolves caught the Sun and ate her.

But since mankind's discovery that the Moon is a cold, dark body that shines only with the reflected light of the Sun, it has been demoted to second place in the heavens, which is, of course, another reason why it is associated with 2. In our society, being 'number two' means that although one has tried, one is not 'first among men' but 'second rate'. It is no coincidence that those who come second in sports events are awarded a silver medal, for silver is the metal of the Moon. Nor is it surprising that the winner gets the gold.

To us the Moon is female, its twenty-eight-day cycle matching that of the female menstrual period and its grace, coolness and aura of mystery the feminine character. So also is 2, which follows 1 and is created from it, just as Eve was fashioned from Adam, the first man. 2 is thus connected with all those traits, foibles, attractions and weaknesses that are characteristically feminine. 1 is bright and hot, 2 is shadowy and cold; 1 is simple and rational, 2 is complex and intuitive; 1 is upright and erect, 2 is curved and smooth. And because all living things, in the ancient view, were created by the divine pairing of earth and sky, 2 is also the number of pregnancy and birth.

Less favourably, 2 represents that which opposes: the contrary, the antagonistic and the enemy. For if 1 symbolizes God, 2 is Satan, the Devil, whose two horns and cloven feet show his numerical standing. And by association 2 is the number of the Left-Hand Path, of night and darkness, of secret things and hidden things, and of witches, warlocks and the undead. 2 is duplicity, untruth, 'speaking with a forked tongue'. It is also the number of passivity, submissiveness, pliability, restraint, and of all that is uncertain and obscure.

Many myths and legends involve that most enigmatic of twosomes, twins. Typically, mythical twins, while born of the same mother, have different fathers, one a god, the other mortal, this difference lying at the root of their subsequent conflict. For twins, again typically, fight each other, with the result that one usually kills the other. Indeed, the quarrel between the Greek twins Proteus and Acrisius began while they were still in the womb.

The myths in which a semi-divine human twin fights his mortal brother are symbolic of the struggles between the worshippers of the celestial twins, the Sun and the Moon, which took place at the dawn of history. To early man the Sun and the Moon were the most obvious and potent celestial objects, whose circular shape and apparent identical size suggested a brotherly relationship, but whose differences of brightness, heat production and times of appearance pointed to an underlying dissimilarity. And while the Sun's dominance of the day and the Moon's of the night suggested that the two brothers had successfully divided the sky between them, each seemed jealous of the other and schemed to snatch his portion of the sky for himself. The Sun's power grew during the spring and summer, when the days lengthened, and Moon's in the autumn and winter, when the nights became longer. Such cosmic contention reached a climax when a solar eclipse occurred, the darkness it brought threatening the end of the world.

The most famous twins in Greek myth are Castor and Polydeuces (or Pollux), the Dioscuri, whose symbol, the *docana*, representing two upright pillars, is still used for Gemini, the sign of the Twins. Polydeuces, being the son of Zeus, is the immortal solar twin, and Castor, the son of an ordinary mortal, is the lunar twin. Castor's name, which means 'beaver', links him with water and wood, both of which are lunar substances. In numerological terms Polydeuces is 1 and Castor 2. The Dioscuri are unusual in that instead of quarrelling with each other, they do so with another pair of twins, Idas and Lynceus, which eventually leads to the two lunar brothers, Castor and Lynceus, being killed by their respective solar opposites.

The Greeks said that the Moon's chariot was drawn by two white horses, as was Eos' (or Dawn's). Both the Moon and 2 are associated with mares, cows and with female animals in general, and with dogs. Orthrus, the two-headed hound of Geryon, was the legendary progenitor of the Sphinx and the Nemean Lion (lions once being sacred to the Moon).

If you were born on the 2nd, the 20th or the 22nd, the influence of 2 is strong in your life and you are, like Castor, a lunar child. The influence of 2 is similarly strong if you were born on the 12th, 21st, 23rd, 24th, 25th, 26th, 27th, 28th or 29th, although the conjoined numbers represent moderating characteristics. Lunar influences are likewise potent in the lives of those born in February, the second month of the year. The Romans associated February with the dead and believed it to be unlucky, which is why they made it the shortest month. Famous people born on the 2nd include Marie Antoinette (2-11-1755), Arthur Bliss (2-8-1891), Edward Elgar (2-6-1857), Nell Gwynn (2-1-1650), Alec Douglas-Home (2-7-1903), Warren Harding (2-11-1865) and the Marquis de Sade (2-6-1740).

Should 2 figure strongly in your birthdate, you are an introverted and thoughtful type, possessing great sensitivity and intuition. If you are a man you probably have a slender, rather feminine physique, one not suited to rough games or physical work. You are the victim of much uncertainty about yourself, which makes you tense and anxious, this in turn preventing you from sleeping well. Your tenseness is exacerbated by the changeable nature of your life, which suggests to you that you are not in control of your destiny. Your lack of confidence makes it hard for you to stick up for yourself or to freely express your point of view. It also adversely affects your relationships.

2 is the number of white and of very pale colours, of bloodlessness, and of intuition and instinct. In the human body it represents fair skin that reacts badly to sunlight, hair that is blonde, lank and fine, weak bones and muscles, worried-looking eyes and a soft-spoken voice. The direction of 2 is south-east, whence travel or residence is favourable for the 2 born. The best times of the year for 2s occur whenever the Moon is lodged in Taurus, where it is exalted, although a waxing Moon is generally good for them. Their worst periods happen when the Moon is located in Scorpio, which is the sign of its debilitation.

A 2 vowel number indicates that you are rather laid-back and repressed, but also that you have creative talents and a strong desire to learn. Others find you hard to get to know because you are not particularly vocal or demonstrative, and they tend to think that you have something to hide. You are quite shy and you lack self-confidence. This makes you a follower, not a leader, and you prefer to suggest rather than instruct. Because you are impressionable, your surroundings have a strong effect on your mood and you are very much influenced by the opinions and actions of others. Security is important to you and this is why you must be very careful when choosing a marriage partner. With someone who gives you the right amount of love and respect you blossom into a warm and delightful human being, but when these are lacking you shrivel up and die inwardly, and you may have self-destructive thoughts. You are a good listener and because you instinctively know where others are going wrong, you give excellent advice. This is why you do very well in fields like counselling, social work and psychiatry, whose aim is to help others. Indeed, your ability to put yourself in another's shoes makes you a natural champion of the poor and oppressed. But because you constantly question your own beliefs and goals, you are your own worst enemy. Thus, it is essential for you to have the support of someone who has the confidence you lack and who can focus both your mind and your energies.

The functioning of your ego personality is helped or hindered by your id nature, which is symbolized by your consonant number. Because odd numbers represent qualities that do not go well with those symbolized by the even numbers, your 2 ego is best served by an id symbolized by 4, 6 or 8, all of which are stronger and more stable than 2. In the solar cycle 2 is opposed by 6, the number of the descended Sun, which is therefore the most compatible id type for you to have.

If your consonant number is 2 you have a very rich and imaginative inner life, which sometimes seems more real than the world around you. You are strongly psychic and you are often troubled by strange dreams and presentiments. Indeed, should you wish to develop these talents you could become a gifted medium or clairvoyant. But if you have an odd ego number, particularly if this is 1, you may ignore these insights and try to repress them, preferring instead to trust to logic. You enjoy reading and artistic activities like painting and drawing, and you rather like being alone. Your 2 id indicates that you were frightened of the dark and of nameless terrors as a child, and that you are prone to nervous disorders and to superstitious fears, which may debilitate you. In your negative periods you are restless and moody, to the extent that others find you unpredictable and unreliable. You dislike responsibility and you will, if you're not careful, drift through life. You have a tendency to change both your job and your residence often. You have a need to serve others, which is why you find nursing, social work, fund-raising and allied work attractive.

If 2 is your name number you are a night person, preferring to stay out late instead of hitting the hay at a reasonable hour. The Moon affects you quite drastically, and you are restless and unsettled at Full Moon. You like salty food, silver jewellery, rainy weather, new clothes, places close to the sea or beside rivers, journeys by boat, the feel of metal and minerals, clean living, religion and positive people. Your lucky day of the week is Monday; your lucky gemstones are the emerald, the moonstone, the ruby and the turquoise; your lucky flowers are the peony, the poppy and the water lily; and your lucky colours are amber, emerald green and white.

The Number 3

3 is the most potent, mysterious and religious of the nine single numbers, for it is the number of the divine force manifesting in human life creatively and procreatively. Folk-tales are replete with threesomes – three wishes, three questions, three truths, three sisters, etc. – and triplets and triads figure extensively in the myths and legends of every age and country. As a holy number 3 appears in Christian belief as the Trinity of Father, Son and Holy Ghost. 'The way begets one,' said the Chinese sage Lao Tzu; 'one begets two; two begets three; three begets the myriad creatures. The myriad creatures carry on their backs the yin and embrace in their arms the yang and are the blending of the generative forces of the two.'

It is probable that 3 became linked with the divine at an early age because in those countries where civilization began – in the Middle East, particularly Egypt – the year had only three seasons, spring, summer and winter, which naturally seemed to represent the three aspects of the generative force, the risen, the whole and the dying god, whose yearly cycle mirrored the daily genesis and nemesis of the Sun as Khepri, Re and Atum.

In Sumerian myth the universe was said to have been created by Enlil, the child of An (heaven) and Ki (earth), forcing apart his copulating parents, while the Egyptians had Shu, who, like Enlil, is the air, separating the similarly entwined Nut (heaven) and Geb (earth), to bring the world into existence. The third entity is thus creative in an active, forceful way, while at the same time being, like the air itself, empty and invisible. Here, surely, is the root of all religion.

In Greek myth Rhea, the earth, gives birth to three sons, Hades, Poseidon and Zeus, who respectively take command of the underworld, the sea and the sky, and three daughters, Hestia, Demeter and Hera. Zeus (the Roman Jupiter), who becomes the king of the gods, is the third son and is nursed by three nymphs.

Together the sons represent the three-season year: Poseidon, whose symbol is the bull, is the deity of the spring; Zeus, whose symbol is the lion, is the deity of the summer; and Hades, symbolized by the serpent, is the god of the winter. Poseidon bears a trident, as did Britannia on the old British penny to symbolize Britain's sea power, and fathers three children on the nymph Amphitrite ('the third one who encircles'), while Tartarus, Hades' realm, is guarded by the three-headed dog Cerberus, and has three regions and a trio of judges, Minos, Rhadamanthys and Aecus, who try the souls of the dead at a place where three roads meet.

Greek mythology also provides us with the three Erinnyes or Furies, who avenge the crimes of parricide and perjury, the three Fates, the three Muses, the three Hesperides, the three Harpies, the three Graeae, the three Gorgons, and Hecate, the third aspect of the Moon and the goddess of witches, who has three bodies and three heads.

In addition to being the number of the divine, 3 also symbolizes intelligence, knowledge, wisdom, creative expression, good living and sexual union for procreative purposes. Astrologically, it is linked with Jupiter, the largest planet of the solar system, and thus with the zodiac signs of Sagittarius and Pisces, which respectively represent the worldly and the spiritual aspects of both Jupiter and 3.

If you were born on the 3rd or the 30th of any month you are strongly influenced by 3, as you are, although less forcibly, if you were born on the 13th, 23rd or 31st. 3 similarly exerts an influence over those born in March, the third month, and December, the twelfth month (1 + 2 = 3). Famous people born on the 3rd include Clement Attlee (3-1-1883), Marlon Brando (3-4-1924), Rupert Brooke (3-8-1887), Felix Mendelssohn (3-2-1809), Dolly Parton (3-1-1946) and Burt Reynolds (3-11-1936). And it was the thrice-married film actress Jean Harlow (3-3-1911) who once said, 'I like to wake up in the morning and feel a new man.'

If 3 is prominent in your birthdate you are tall and strong-boned with a tendency to run to fat. You have a hearty appetite and a love of good food and drink. You are sociable and convivial, and you enjoy making whoopee. Because you are an extrovert you don't like being alone, which is why you would rather associate with dubious types than spend an evening without company. You are basically a cheery, open and frank person, who likes to spend money and gamble. Yet you have a spiritual side and a psychic's sensitivity. You enjoy learning and you are naturally attracted to teaching, law, journalism and the arts.

3 is the number of purple, the imperial colour, and of brown and yellow. This is why 3 people often have a blotchy complexion, which is caused by their over-indulgence in rich food and strong drink. Typically, 3's have rather plump, full faces, long noses and a lot of fine, healthy hair. The direction of 3 is to the south, and residence or travel in that direction is fortunate for 3s. Their best period takes place when Jupiter transits the zodiac sign of Cancer, where it is exalted, their worst when Jupiter passes through Capricorn, where it is debilitated. Jupiter will return to Cancer on 5 August 1989, and will remain in the sign for a little over a year, until 19 August 1990. It won't be back in Capricorn until 4 January 1996, and because it will stay in the sign until 22 January 1997, the year 1996 will be a rather difficult one for 3s.

If your ego personality is symbolized by a 3 vowel number, you are an extroverted, friendly and likeable soul. You have a lot of confidence, although you do occasionally experience periods of uncertainty, when you may drink too heavily or abuse your body in other ways. In fact, you don't take very good care of yourself, especially in the middle part of your life when you risk becoming flabby and out of shape. You are easily bored and this may prompt you to change your job quite often in an effort to find something that can stimulate and challenge you. You enjoy the outdoors and you are a keen sportsman, although typically as a spectator rather than as a participant. You are frank, honest and forthright, and you expect others to be similarly open. Indeed, you despise the hypocrite and the dissembler. Because you are quite humorous and optimistic, you are popular. You possess musical and artistic gifts, and you love to learn. You are also a natural teacher, with an enthusiasm for transmitting knowledge that is infectious. You like money and all that it can buy, yet despite your materialism you sense that there is a dimension of the spirit which not only attracts you but which helps guard you against excess. Being independent, you like to play the field in love and you certainly won't rush into marriage.

Because 3 represents the Sun at noon, when it has reached its zenith, your ego is best served by an id whose qualities are symbolized by 7, the number of both the Sun at its nadir and the waning Moon. Other odd numbered ids also serve you well, but if you have an id represented by 2, 4, 6 or 8 you will be less confident, shyer and more troubled, although your creativity and psychic ability will be greater.

If you have an id symbolized by 3 you feel different from your fellows, mainly because you recognize the presence of the divine in your life. Indeed, religion is important to you and quite probably you are a regular church-goer. You may even have thought about entering the ministry. Your id, however, is its own worst enemy because although it tries to act as your spiritual guardian, it is also the source of your strong sexual urges, thus it constantly tempts your ego with erotic images only to condemn it – and so making you feel guilty and ashamed – when you give way to temptation. Because 3 is the most intuitive of the odd numbers, your id from time to time gives you amazing insights and prophetic dreams, although the use you make of these depends very much on your ego. While you try to behave in a mature and responsible way, both in your work and at home, you periodically have lapses, when you act foolishly and out of character. At such times you tend to take unnecessary risks, such as gambling money you can ill-afford to lose. Indeed, you rather like betting and occasionally – but not always – you are blessed with incredible luck.

Should 3 be your name number you love the open air, driving in fast cars, hiking and cycling, and attending sports events. Because you are a night person, you don't like rising early. You are fond of animals, sweet foods, expensive clothes and furnishings, children, fruit and orchards, churches, cathedrals and holy places generally, and cultivated people. Your lucky day of the week is Thursday; your lucky gemstones are the amethyst, the sapphire and the turquoise; your lucky flowers are the carnation, the pimpernel and the wallflower; and your lucky colours are blue, mauve, orange and purple.

The Number 4

4 is the number of the Negative Sun and it is the second of the Sun's two numbers. The Sun is given two numbers because its daily and its yearly cycles are divided into two. During the morning the Sun rises into the sky to reach its zenith at noon, from where it descends to vanish finally beneath the horizon. Likewise, during the first half of the year, through the spring and summer, the Sun gains height and grows hotter, while in the autumn and winter it steadily loses altitude and gives less heat. In fact, during both cycles the Sun waxes and wanes. 1 is therefore the number of the waxing Sun, symbolized by the lion, and 4 is the number of the

waning Sun, whose animal symbol is the serpent.

In Greek myth the Sun-god Helius' chariot is pulled by four white horses, while that of Hades, the first son of Rhea, who can be identified with both the waning Sun and the Sun which has sunk beneath the horizon, is drawn by four black horses. The ancient anxieties generated by the Sun's nightly disappearance lie behind the myth of Theseus' and Peirithous' descent into Tartarus, where Hades confines them for four years. Theseus (whose name means 'he who lays down') represents the setting Sun and Peirithous ('he who turns around') the rising Sun. It is no coincidence that the two men are released from Tartarus by Heracles, the archetypal solar hero.

Because 4 is the number of the waning Sun and of the Sun at night, it is linked with inward and hidden things, with death and the afterlife, and with the earth and the treasures of the earth. 4 is also the number of divine revelation – Helius being the god of divination – and of stability and fertility. This is perhaps why Lao Tzu said, 'Within the realm there are four things that are great . . . the way is great; heaven is great; earth is great; and the king also is great.'

Greek myth records that Zeus fathered four of the Olympian deities – Hermes, Apollo, Artemis and Dionysus – out of wedlock; that Artemis practised four times with the silver bow made for her by the Cyclopes; that the Sphinx, child of the two-headed hound Orthrus, had a body made from the parts of four different creatures; and that Peleus was given four wedding gifts, a spear, a suit of golden armour, and two horses.

Important tetrads include the four temperate seasons, the four points of the year (the two solstices and the two equinoxes), the four elements, the four humours, the four winds, the four cardinal virtues and the four letters of the Tetragrammaton, YHVH, which represent the secret name of God.

Marduk, the Babylonian god of lightning, the flood-storm and the four winds, who was all-seeing and all-hearing, possessed a double number of sense organs:

> Four were his eyes, four were his ears;
> When he moved his lips, fire blazed forth.
> Large were all four hearing organs,
> And the eyes, in like number, scanned all things.

If you were born on the 4th of any month the influence of 4 is strong in your life; it is also important if you were born on the 14th or the 24th. Indeed, the 14th is a very special birthdate because it is made up of both the Sun's numbers, 1 and 4, and those whose birthday it is have demonstrable light and dark sides, which were evident in photographer Cecil Beaton's (14-1-1904) job, the morals of Frank Harris (14-2-1856), and the life of Che Guevara (14-6-1928), who said: 'In a revolution one wins or dies.' 4 is likewise important in the lives of the April born, for April is the fourth month of the year. The Romans held celebrations in honour of Magna Mater, the Great Mother, that is, the earth, on 4 April. Famous people with birthdays on the 4th include Anton Bruckner (4-9-1824), Calvin Coolidge (4-7-1872), Queen Elizabeth, the Queen Mother (4-8-1900), Charles Lindbergh (4-2-1902) and Clyde Tombaugh (4-2-1906), the discoverer of Pluto.

If 4 is well represented in your birthdate you are a reticent person with a good sense of humour and a calm, steady demeanour, both of which belie a rather rough, aggressive and volatile inner you that is only shown when you are angered or pushed too far. You are quite tall and have a strong, muscular body and regular features. You are not as confident in yourself as you would like to be, and you suffer from periods of self-doubt and anxiety, which you keep carefully hidden. You enjoy working hard and you see nothing wrong in wealth and luxury as long as they have been earned. Although others find you difficult to get to know, you are a faithful friend once your friendship has been won. You are honest and law-abiding, and you believe in fair play.

The colour of 4 is brown, the colour of the soil, but it is also linked with lighter and brighter colours, such as blue and violet. Similarly, the colouring of 4 people is either dark (the colour of the Negative Sun) or light (the colour of the Positive Sun). The physique may also be tall and slim or short and stout. One characteristic feature of 4's is the Greek nose, which lacks an indentation between the nose bridge and the forehead. The direction of 4 is to the south-west, and travel or residence in that part of the country or globe is fortunate for 4s. Like 1s, 4 individuals find life easiest when the Sun transits Aries, which it does every year between 20 March and 20 April, and most difficult when it passes through Libra, which it does annually between 24 September and 23 October.

If 4 is your vowel number you have a strong and stable ego and you are generally responsible and dependable. Yet you are not as confident or as well adjusted as you would wish, and you are plagued by periodic bouts of self-doubt and uncertainty. You are unusual in that while you need to live a structured life, you also like change and variety, which means that you are happiest working freelance or at a job that allows you a good deal of freedom and the opportunity to travel. Should your work or your home life prove too restricting you will suffer in silence for a long while before suddenly and dramatically breaking away, to pick up the pieces elsewhere. Indeed, such volcanic changes are typical of the 4 character. You can work quite well with others, although you don't much like taking orders. Because you are creative and clever with your hands, you are naturally attracted to music and art and to jobs which combine creativity with practical application, such as that of the architect, engineer and designer. You are friendly, yet your need to remain independent makes you somewhat aloof, which is why you have more acquaintances than friends. You were rather moody and difficult when young, and you can still plunge into unfathomable silences, much to everyone's puzzlement. You don't give much away about yourself, which gives you a certain mystery. Your pleasures tend to be on the unusual side, so allowing you to get out of yourself, thus you're more likely to be learning kung-fu or going scuba-diving than playing golf. Marriage doesn't appeal to you all that much and you will try to put it off for as long as you decently can.

Your 4 ego is moderated by your id, whose character and state is represented by the consonant number of your name. Because 4 is an even number, you are best served by an even-numbered id, for otherwise your ego's stability will be constantly threatened by restless urges from below. An 8 id is most compatible with a 4 ego, because such an id is balanced and comparatively quiescent. 2, 4 and 6 id types are also compatible, but less so than an 8 id. Of course, a 4 id is essentially the same as a 4 ego: it won't create problems but it won't provide stimulant pressures either. Less favourable are ids represented by the odd numbers 1, 3, 5, 7 and 9, although 1 ids, being solar by nature, have natural affinities with 4 egos that the others lack.

A 4 consonant number reveals that you have an id rich in creative ideas and intuitive awareness, which makes you something of a primary source when it comes to producing brainwaves and insights. Yet despite this you are noted for your stubborn persistence, thus you don't find it easy to alter course once you have started something. However, if you have a less persistent and rather contrary ego number, a 4 id will act as a positive counterweight, helping you keep your nose to the grindstone. You are concerned about the state of the world and about the lot of your fellow man, which is why you tend to give to charities and protest against things like seal hunting and nuclear waste disposal. Ideally, you like to live in quiet, pleasant surroundings, and you need the support and respect of your colleagues and friends. Yet, ironically, security makes you feel uneasy because you sense that it could trap you. This is why you are always planning travel trips and activities that are different and exotic.

If your name number is 4 you reach your daily peak in the afternoon and early evening. You dress oddly and somewhat unconventionally, and you are generous where big sums of money are involved but mean with small expenditures. You like dry river beds and salt flats, pottery items and watching pots being made, birds, plants, especially shrubs, and you have a penchant for the occult. Your lucky day of the week is Saturday; your lucky gemstones are the amethyst, the aquamarine and the lapis lazuli; your lucky flowers are the buttercup, the fennel and the foxglove; and your lucky colours are electric blue and green, brown, violet and off-white.

The Number 5

The number 5 is perhaps the most interesting of the nine single numbers, not least because it is the number of sexual pleasure, deception and magic. Astrologically, 5 is the number of the planet Mercury and the setting Sun. Mercury is identified with the setting Sun because, lying so near the Sun, it only becomes visible just after sunset. In Greek and Roman mythology Mercury (or Hermes) is the god who conducts the souls of the dead to the underworld and he was originally the god of the twilight. In Tartarus Mercury delivers the ghosts to Charon, the ferryman, who rows them across the black waters of the river Styx. In keeping with Mercury's numerological associations, the Styx has five tributaries: Acheron, Phlegethon, Cocytus, Aornis and Lethe.

Mercury's mother is Maia, one of the Pleiades nymphs, who were pursued by Orion for five years before being transformed into stars. Maia gave her name to May, the fifth month, during which the Pleiades rise with the Sun to mark the start of the nautical year. This is probably why Mercury became the god of mariners. In fact, Mercury's jurisdiction was wide, as befits his restless character, and he was the god of invention, soothsaying, musicianship, treaties, trade and commerce, theft, travel, artifice and mathematics. He was also the messenger of Zeus. Mercury wears winged sandals and carries a magic wand with which he can induce sleep.

Additionally, as the god of intelligence, speech and communication, Mercury was credited with the invention of the alphabet, which has five vowels, while the five fingers of the hand link both Mercury and the number 5 with manual skills. Indeed, the right hand symbolizes Mercury as an Olympian deity, this being the hand with which most of us write, throw dice, strum a musical instrument, seal bargains, etc., while the left, the awkward or sinister hand, is the hand of Mercury as conductor of the dead.

The names of the five fingers of the right hand derive from those of the five male Dactyls who sprang into life when Rhea, giving birth to Zeus, dug her fingers into the ground. Each finger of the right hand is also identified with one of the vowels of the alphabet. The thumb is the digit of the vowel A and is named Heracles; the index finger, that of O, is named Paeonis; the middle finger, that of U, is named Epimedes; the third finger, that of E, is named Iasius; and the little finger, which palmists link specifically with Mercury, is that of the vowel I and is called Acesidas. In a similar manner the thumb is identified with the winter solstice, when the Sun is reborn, the index finger with the spring equinox, the middle finger with the summer solstice, the third finger with the autumn equinox, and the little finger with the winter solstice again, when the Sun dies. In the ancient tree alphabet, A, the vowel of the thumb, was the first letter, and I, the vowel of the little finger, the last. This old alphabet is recalled in the expression 'from A to Izzard', meaning from start to finish, 'Izzard' being a variant of Z.

The names of the five female Dactyls who are personified by the fingers of the left hand have been lost, probably because their repetition was considered unlucky.

The hands can thus be considered as representing the polarities of nature, the right hand being the male and hence symbolizing light, logic, dexterity, action, openness, etc. – that is, the good, and the left the female, or darkness, intuition, clumsiness, passiveness, concealment, etc. – in other words, the bad.

As Hermes Trismegistus – Hermes 'three times very, very great' – Mercury was said to have introduced astrology and its philosophical system, which is summed up by the dictum 'as above, so below', to mankind.

Astrology interprets the movements of the five planets and the two lights, the Sun and the Moon, in terms of human destiny. It is not surprising, therefore, to find that the fingers and the other parts of the hand – the hands being the bodily parts by which man imposes his will on the world – are linked with these celestial bodies. The thumb is the digit of Venus; the index finger, Jupiter; the middle finger, Saturn; the third finger, the Sun; and the little finger, Mercury.

But despite 5's close association with Mercury and his many attributes, the number never became as important in the West as it did in China, where, no doubt because of the special attention given to the five planets, 5 was the only number worthy of serious study. The Chinese recognized five zones of space, five odours, five musical notes, five human senses, five vital facial features, five metals, five duties, five elements, five colours, five directions and a plethora of other fives, each fifth part of which was ruled by one of the five planets. Mercury, for example, was the planet of the element *water*, the metal *iron*, the colour *black*, and the direction *north*. The other planets were linked with the following elements, metals, colours and directions.

	Element	*Metal*	*Colour*	*Direction*
VENUS	Metal	Silver	White	West
MARS	Fire	Copper	Red	South
JUPITER	Wood	Lead	Blue	East
SATURN	Earth	Gold	Yellow	Centre

In fact, the Chinese were so five-minded that they saw 5 wherever they looked, which is perhaps why the sage Lao Tzu warned, 'The five colours make a man's eyes blind; the five notes make his ears deaf; the five tastes injure his palate.'

But although 5 symbolizes intelligence, cleverness and versatility, it is also the number of instability, irresponsibility and indeterminancy, which is why it has been called the Errol Flynn of numbers. Thus, it is perhaps hardly surprising that 5 turns up with alarming frequency in the names and birthdates of those who are sexually promiscuous or sexually abnormal, or criminally predisposed or psychologically disturbed. 5 is the number of genius, but genius is next to madness.

The influence of 5 is strong in your life if you were born on the 5th, as it is, but to a lesser degree, if your birthday is the 15th or the 25th. The addition of 1 and 2 to the birthdate gives 5 a stability it lacks on its own. New projects, for instance, are often successfully launched on the 15th, such as the founding of the McDonald's hamburger chain (15-4-1955), the launch of decimalization in Britain (15-2-1971), and the publication of Sir Isaac Pitman's Stenographic Sound-hand book (15-11-1837). The 5th, by contrast, saw the arrest of Oscar Wilde for homosexuality (5-4-1895), the assassination of Robert Kennedy (5-6-1968), and the start of the unsuccessful Sino-Soviet talks (5-7-1963) which led to the rift between the two countries. Because 5 is the number of May, the fifth month, those born in May tend to be rather restless and footloose. Famous people with birthdays on the 5th include Walt Disney (5-12-1901), Henry II of England (5-3-1133), John Huston (5-8-1906), Tatum O'Neal (5-11-1963) and Sir Robert Peel (5-2-1788).

If 5 is prominent in your birthdate you are likely to be of slender build, 5 being the number of the ectomorph. Quite possibly you would like to be heavier than you are, but find it difficult to put on weight. Your gauntness stems from your high metabolic rate, which readily burns up what you eat. You also tend not to bother about eating regularly. Although you are generally outgoing and cheerful, your natural anxiety and impatience sometimes makes you irritable and short-tempered, to the detriment of your relationships. You suffer periodic bouts of moodiness and almost manic restlessness, especially during your twenties and thirties. You have a clear speaking voice and a love of words. Indeed, you are an effective communicator. You also like reading and writing. You are blessed with a good sense of humour and you enjoy playing jokes and making others laugh.

The colour of 5 is yellow, which, being close to gold, reflects Mercury's proximity to the Sun. 5 people frequently have a sallow complexion, a yellowness that also tends to appear in the white of the eyes and on the teeth. The typical 5 person has a thin, long-limbed body, straight, fine hair, thin eyebrows and lips, weak teeth, and quick, restless movements. The direction of 5 is west, whence travel or residence is fortunate for 5s. All 5 types find life easier for them when Mercury transits the zodiac sign of Virgo, where it is exalted, and at a low ebb when the little planet passes through Pisces, where it is debilitated. Because Mercury usually spends no more than about one month in each sign, it returns to Virgo every year.

If 5 is the vowel number of your name, you have a 5 ego and a personality to match. This means that you have a clever mind which enables you to learn new skills and absorb facts quickly. However, your mental sharpness makes you rather impatient with those less able than yourself. You love to talk and argue – especially the latter – and you are good at languages. Because you enjoy a challenge, you readily tackle any problem that comes your way, even though you may not be qualified to solve it. You like games such as chess and backgammon, which enable you to pit your wits against an opponent, but not rough, body contact games, such as rugby or football. You are not, however, blessed with much persistence, thus you often give up if you can't solve a problem or get your own way easily or quickly. You have a persuasive tongue, which allows you to manipulate others, and a good sense of humour. But although your knowledge is wide, you tend to know a little about a lot. Because you are quick, light and funny you find it easy to meet people and as a result you have an active and interesting social life. Yet you have few close friends because any emotional commitment scares you. You keep your own emotions under tight control, to the extent that your friends and colleagues seldom know what you are really feeling. You tend to be neurotic, and if typical, you pay too much attention to your appearance and to the tidiness of your home. Indeed, dirt and dust make you uncomfortable and angry, as do slovenly habits. You also worry too much about your health and you are something of a sucker for quack remedies. While you are both attractive to and interested in the opposite sex, you shy away from serious commitment and may flit from one relationship to the next. Also, you have a tendency to kiss and tell, which can hurt your ex-partners. Fortunately, however, sex is not all that important to you. What you like is the chase!

Because 5 represents the setting Sun, poised on the brink of the abyss, your 5 ego is perhaps the most unstable of the ego types and it takes relatively little to push you 'over the edge'. This is why you need to have a stable id, for this will provide a psychic counterweight to your natural restlessness and impatience. In this respect the numbers of the rising Sun – 1 and 9 – are ideal consonant numbers for you, for such an id will balance your ego. 3 and 7 consonant numbers likewise indicate a favourable id. However, a 5 id is not suitable for a 5 ego and should you have such an id you will find it hard to cope. Ids represented by the even numbers – 2, 4, 6 and 8 – suggest that you are at odds with your emotions and that you tend to suffer from self-doubt and depression.

If your consonant number is 5, your id is very much a thorn in your side because it constantly throws up all manner of restless, critical and exotic ideas and images, which make it difficult for you to feel at peace with yourself. It continually says, 'Come on! Get up, get out and get going!' so pressurizing you to run in all directions at once. Of course, such an id is stimulating and even positive if you have an ego that can successfully channel its demands, but if not it will prompt a lot of silly desires and irrational actions. At its best, a 5 id gives you a love of learning, travel and adventure, an interest in progress and change, and a talent for social intercourse. Because it is oddly in tune with natural forces, your id can warn you of future dangers and tell you if someone is trying to con you. If you're wise you'll trust your hunches – but not when you're near a roulette wheel or a racetrack. You do like to gamble and this can cause you a lot of problems with your finances. In a similar way, your 5 id encourages you to put up a false front behind which you hide your real self.

If 5 is your name number you like public places, gossip, going to the theatre, listening to music and finding things out. Your best time of the day is early evening, and you love watching the Sun go down. The autumn is your favourite season. You enjoy spending time in gardens, walking in the rain, watching birds, eating different foods, sitting beneath leafy trees, and the company of your maternal uncles. Your lucky day of the week is Wednesday; your lucky gemstones are the agate, Alexandrite, the opal and the onyx; your lucky flowers are the gladiolus, the orchid and the snapdragon; and your lucky colours are light green, orange and yellow.

The Number 6

The number 6 is undoubtedly the most attractive of the nine single numbers because it symbolizes love and marriage, birth and growth, and peace. Its planet is Venus, who in mythology was the goddess of love. Yet in the solar cycle 6 is the number of the descended Sun, poised mid-way between its setting and its nadir. This indicates that 6 has a dark side to it, that its presence as a birth number or as a name number does not always augur happiness. Indeed, love as often brings pain as it does pleasure, and the divorce statistics speak eloquently of the problems and difficulties of marriage.

Like 3, which symbolizes the male sex urge and procreation, 6 is the number of female sexuality, children and family life. It is also the number of simplicity, neatness, hard work, happiness and art.

The generative nature of 6 is illustrated by the biblical account of God's creation of the world and everything in it in six days, and in myth by the Greek goddess Rhea giving birth to six children, three of whom were male and three female, and by the story in the Epic of Gilgamesh of how Enkidu, the wild man, was tamed by a harlot after six days of sexual passion, which gave him wisdom and put 'the thoughts of man . . . in his heart.' Heroic acts are rarely associated with 6: Theseus' departure for Crete, where he slew the Minotaur, on 6 April, being but one of the few examples.

In very ancient times the goddess of the planet Venus had a dual character and a dual role: she was both the amorous and enticing Queen of Love and the destructive and murderous Lady of Battles. This duality derived from the planet Venus' appearance in the sky as either the morning star or the evening star, the former representing the goddess in her benign aspect, the latter the goddess in her warlike aspect. Indeed, Venus was known as the 'Star of Lamentation' when it shone at night.

Venus was called Inanna by the Sumerians. Her brother and husband was Utu, the Sun, a relationship suggested by the planet Venus' proximity to that body, and her sister was Ereshkigal, the Queen of the Underworld. One myth describes how Inanna descends into Ereshkigal's realm to liberate her lover Dumuzi, the god of the harvest, who had been imprisoned there. Angered by Inanna's insolent intrusion into the land of death, Ereshkigal captures her and subjects her to the ravages of sixty illnesses. She remains in the nether world until Utu and Nanna, the Moon, get help from Enki, the god of the planet Jupiter, who secures her release.

This descent of Venus/Inanna into the underworld explains why 6 occupies the position that is does in the solar cycle, a placement that also symbolizes Venus as the feared goddess of war, who despatches the souls of slain warriors to Tartarus.

In our discussion of the number 3 we noted how God or 'the divine' is often represented by a triad of male deities. This threesome typically becomes increased to six by the gods' marriage to their sisters, a doubling which reveals why 6 symbolizes both marriage and family life. Thus, the trio of Babylonian high gods – Anu, Enlil and Ea – marry, respectively, their sisters Antu, Ninlil and Ninki. This incestuous union must also have originally taken place between the six children of Rhea, but because the Greeks came to abhor such marriages, only Zeus' marriage to Hera was allowed to stand. Yet there is evidence that

Poseidon was once the spouse of his sister Demeter, and Hades of Hestia.

However, despite the close association of 6 with Venus, its appearance in Greek myth is infrequent. It generally occurs only as numbers of children. For example, the Greeks said that Poseidon fathered six sons of the nymph Halia; that Aeolus, the guardian of the winds, had six sons and six daughters by his wife Enarete; and that Apollo killed six of Niobe's seven sons and his sister, Artemis, six of her daughters. It is, however, worth remembering that the first Olympian family consisted of six gods, Zeus, Poseidon, Apollo, Hermes, Hephaistos and Ares, and six goddesses, Hera, Demeter, Artemis, Athene, Aphrodite and Hestia. This company of double sixes was only altered when Dionysus, the god of wine, took the place of the self-effacing Hestia, the goddess of the hearth. Hades, being the god of the underworld, was never an Olympian.

If you were born on the 6th of any month the influence of 6 is strong in your life, as it is, although to a lesser degree, if your birthday falls on the 16th or the 26th. 6 is also a potent factor in the lives of those born in June, the sixth month. The name June derives from Juno, the Roman goddess of marriage, who had the power to make a marriage both happy and fertile. Famous people with birthdays on the 6th include the German composer Max Bruch (6-1-1838), Henry VI of England (6-12-1421), Robert Mitchum (6-8-1917), Ronald Reagan (6-2-1911) and baseball player 'Babe' Ruth (6-2-1895).

If 6 is well represented in your birthdate, you are probably quite tall, although the height of 6 people is very variable. You have an attractive, well-proportioned body, but because you gain weight easily, you have to work at keeping your figure. Your manner is pleasant and friendly and although you are rather introverted, you enjoy the company of others. You don't, however, like being with noisy or ill-mannered people. Yet despite having a lot of friends, your friendships are not very close or enduring, chiefly because you are too selfish and opportunistic where others are concerned. When alone you like reading or listening to music, and you may play a musical instrument or have some other artistic hobby. You are happiest in your home, which is the most important place in your life. If you are not yet married you will certainly be looking forward to the day when you are. You enjoy spending money on clothes and cosmetics, because you think it is important to be attractive to the opposite sex.

6 is the number of green, the colour of plant life. 6 people are blessed with regular features, clear skin and silky, light-coloured hair. Their most beautiful facial feature are their large and lustrous eyes. The direction of 6 is to the north-west, and travel or residence in that direction is fortunate for the 6 born. The best period for them is when Venus transits the zodiacal sign of Pisces, where it is exalted, the worst when Venus transits Virgo, the sign of its debilitation. Because Venus generally stays in each zodiac sign for about a month, it passes through both Pisces and Virgo once every year.

Should you possess a 6 vowel number, symbolizing your ego, you have a well-balanced personality, one that stands on the mid-line between extroversion and introversion. You are naturally reserved, polite and diffident, yet when the mood takes you or the moment is right you can party with the best of them. You feel happiest in surroundings that are bright, colourful and tastefully furnished. You hate dirt and untidiness, and you will go to great lengths to stay clean and neat. Because the notion of balance is important to you, you avoid people and situations that are controversial or upsetting. Indeed, you are both fair and honest, and you believe that the rule of law is central to civilized life. Thus you support the police, order and strong government. However, you dislike injustice, particularly social injustice, and you will always protest against it. But although you have strong views, your ability to see things from the other's point of view stops you from becoming blinkered, thus you are often unsure of your ground when the time comes to cast your vote. In this respect you are a fence-sitter. You are generally careful in your handling of money, although the urge to gamble, to gain riches without effort, can sometimes get the better of you. Because you have an attractive appearance and manner you are popular with the opposite sex, hence you are seldom without a partner of some sort. But you are less successful at ending relationships than beginning them, simply because you find it hard to make a clean break.

An ego symbolized by 6, the number of the Sun mid-way between its setting and its nadir, is best served by an id symbolized by 2, the number of the mid-morning Sun. However, an id represented by any of the even numbers – 2, 4, 6 and 8 – will satisfactorily complement a 6 ego, although a 6 id won't provide the contrast and stimulation that the other id types will. Ids symbolized by the odd numbers – 1, 3, 5, 7 and 9 – will create difficulties because they will rob you of your equanimity by presenting you with all sorts of troublesome feelings and ideas.

If you have a 6 id the deeper levels of your mind are calmer than most, and in your quiet moments you have an inner sense of harmony and peace. You may practise meditation and be interested in mystical and philosophical teachings. A stable, happy home situation is very important to you and you suffer a great deal if things are wrong for you in this respect. This is why the best part of travelling for you is the returning home. Likewise, your strong urge to marry and settle down means that although you may decide to travel, achieve some educational goal or make a career for yourself, you won't feel whole until you have a mate, a home and one or two children. Your id tends to make you resistant to change, thus you are by nature very conservative. However, you will always support changes that right a wrong. You like art and you have an eye for line, form and colour. Indeed, you are creative yourself. Your worst faults are your self-absorption, your vacillation and your tendency to manipulate others.

If 6 is your name number you enjoy the outdoors, especially those places where cereals are grown or where cattle are pastured, or where there are trees. Summer is your favourite season. You also like shops and window-gazing for bargains. Somewhat oddly, you have a taste for sour foods. You like eating out, going to the theatre or cinema, and talking to clergymen. You also like singing, reading poetry, smelling nice, wearing jewellery and colourful clothes, and flowers. Your lucky day of the week is Friday; your lucky gemstones are the chrysolite, the jade and the opal; your lucky flowers are the violet and the white rose; and your lucky colours are blue, emerald green and violet.

The Number 7

There is no doubt that 7 is generally considered to be the most intriguing, mysterious and fortunate of the nine single numbers. And to us in the West the world seems full of sevens, just as it appeared replete with fives to the Chinese. Our heptads include the seven wonders of the world, the seven seas, the seven continents, the seven colours of the rainbow, the seven notes of a musical scale, the seven days of the week, the seven league boots, the seven churches, the seven champions of Christendom, the seven seals, the seven stars, the seven angels and the seven pillars of wisdom.

But this positive view of 7 is not generally met with in

mythology or suggested by 7's astrological associations. 7 is the number of the Negative Moon and of the Sun at its nadir, the lowest point of its cycle, which links it with darkness and the land of the dead.

The ancient myths reveal that 7 was associated with rest, sleep, peace and death at the earliest of times. In Genesis, for example, we learn that God, having created the world in six days, 'rested on the seventh day from all his work that he had made'. A similar cessation of divine activity on the seventh day is recounted by Utnapishtim, the hero of the flood, in the Epic of Gilgamesh. Describing the deluge Utnapishtim says,

> For six days and six nights the winds blew, torrent and tempest and flood overwhelmed the world, tempest and flood raged together like warring hosts. When the seventh day dawned the storm from the south subsided, the sea grew calm, the flood was stilled; I looked at the face of the world and there was silence, all mankind was turned to clay.

And Greek myth recounts the strange story of the twins Agamedes and Trophonius, who were advised by the oracle of Apollo to 'live merrily and indulge yourselves in every pleasure for six days; on the seventh, your heart's desire shall be granted.' On that day Agamedes and Trophonius died quietly in their beds.

It is therefore perhaps hardly surprising to find that the Babylonian underworld contains almost as many heptads as the Greek Tartarus does triads. Ereshkigal's dark realm is surrounded by seven walls, and access to it is only gained by passing through seven gates, each of which is secured by seven bolts. Because every soul has to remove one article of clothing at each gate, so as to arrive naked in the underworld, seven divestments have to be made. And once there the dead are judged by the seven Annunaki.

It was earlier pointed out that both 2 and 7 are identified with the Moon, 2 being the number of the waxing Moon and thus of growth, expansion, moistness, health and life, and 7 the number of the waning Moon, that is, of reduction, shrinkage, dryness, sickness and death. Also 2, being even, is a female number, while 7 being odd, is male. These correspondences indicate that 2 and 7 stand for the opposites of existence, the Yin and the Yang.

But while we with our numerate sophistication can readily accept that because 2 precedes 7 in the number sequence it should be identified with the first, rather than the second phase of the Moon's cycle, we would be wrong in assuming that the ancients cerebrated so simply. Indeed, their close association of 2 with life and 7 with death suggests that they had a much stronger argument for this than the mere fact that 2 lies before 7 in the number sequence. Their reasons must surely have been based on their observations of the natural world, which provided them with the examples of power, change and contrast that formed the framework of their religion.

In Sumer and Babylonia both the Moon and the Sun were worshipped as powerful gods. Each was regarded as an all-seeing deity, who knew the secrets of mankind. There is also evidence of early Moon worship in Egypt, where the Moon may have once been ranked as equal to the Sun, the immortal Re. Indeed, the Sun's and the Moon's equality and their all-seeing power is suggested by the fact that the Egyptians believed them to be the two eyes of Horus, the falcon god, the Sun being Horus' right eye, the Moon his left.

The idea of the Sun and Moon being eyes forms part of a very ancient creation myth, which told how the world was made from the bodily parts of a gigantic god, who had been murdered and dismembered. Echoes of this gruesome story occur in the myth of Uranus, the Greek sky-god, who was castrated by his son Cronus – and who was, incidentally, his seventh son – and from whose blood were created the three Furies and the ash nymphs, the goddess Aphrodite arising from the foam that collected around Uranus' genitals, which Cronus threw into the sea. Somewhat similarly, Egyptian myth records the dismemberment of Osiris by Seth, who then scattered his bodily parts around the land of Egypt.

Fortunately, however, a complete version of this creation myth is found in Scandinavian folklore, which tells us that the first sentient being was the giant Ymir, who is spontaneously created by the interaction of ice and fire. Not long afterwards the god Buri is generated by the divine cow Avonhumla licking salty ice blocks. Buri then gives life to Bor, who in turn fathers the three gods Odin, Vili and Ve. These three kill Ymir and cut him up to create the world – 'From his blood the seas and lakes, from his flesh the earth, and from his bones the mountains; from his teeth and jaws and such bones as were broken they formed the rocks and the pebbles.'

What is particularly interesting about this Norse myth is the fact that the three gods fashion the sky from Ymir's skull, placing it over the earth to create the vault of heaven. In this way Ymir's eyes become the Sun and the Moon.

A living human head has five visible openings: two ears, two nostrils and a mouth. A skull, however, shows two more, the orbits or eye sockets, giving a total of seven (an eighth, the *foramen magnum*, through which passes the spinal cord, can only be seen if the skull is detached from the backbone). It was this number of skull openings which surely suggested to ancient man, to whom the skull was the most potent symbol of death and mortality, that 7 and death are linked, and that the number is also associated with sleep, peace and darkness.

Likewise, 7 is also the number of wisdom and occult knowledge, of thought and learning, and of the unconscious mind.

Since the Sun traditionally represents the right eye and the Moon the left, the question naturally arises as to whether the other skull openings are linked with the five planets. This indeed is the case. Astrology gives Jupiter rulership of the right ear and Saturn of the left ear. Mars likewise governs the right nostril, Venus the left. And Mercury, as might be expected, is the lord of the mouth.

The influence of 7 is strong in your life if you were born on the 7th, as it is, although to a lesser extent, if you were born on the 17th. A birthday on the 27th introduces both lunar numbers into your life, thus making you a distinct Moon person. You are powerfully affected by the Moon, to the extent that your moods and the very pattern of your life ebb and flow in a cyclical manner. 7 is also an important influence in the lives of those born in July, the seventh month. July was named after Julius Caesar, the Roman emperor, at whose death a comet appeared and shone for seven days. Famous people with birthdays on the 7th include Gary Cooper (7-5-1901), Charles Dickens (7-2-1812), Queen Elizabeth I of England (7-9-1533), Billy Graham (7-11-1918), Billie Holiday (7-4-1915), Gustav Mahler (7-7-1860) and Ringo Starr (7-7-1940).

You probably are not very tall if 7 is well represented in your birthdate, and you are likely to be on the plump side. Indeed, your metabolism is slow, which explains why you easily gain weight, a tendency aggravated by your liking for rich foods and alcohol. You probably suffered quite badly from acne and other skin disorders during adolescence, and you may still wish that your complexion was better. You have a poor dress sense, which is not helped by your odd shape, thus you never really look or feel as smart as you would like. But if your appearance needs work, your personality could hardly be bettered, for you are a gentle, friendly and pleasant soul, who has a liking for others and an intuitive understanding of them. Although you are not very ambitious, you place a high value on education. Your main weakness is your tendency to turn to drink or drugs when faced with life's problems.

The colour of 7 is blue, the colour of tropical seas and the sky. 7 people have rather plump facial features and short necks, but are blessed with very attractive eyes. Their foreheads are full and wide and their hair is fine and dark. The direction of 7 is north, and travel or residence in that direction is fortunate for 7 people. The best period for 7s, as it is also for 2s, occurs when the Moon is lodged in the zodiac sign of Taurus, where it is exalted, and the worst is when the Moon is placed in Scorpio, where it is debilitated. Such lunar placements last for about two days every month and their dates can be found by consulting an ephemeris.

If 7 is your vowel number, symbolizing your ego or manifest personality, you are a bright, quite creative type, whose biggest fault, in terms of getting ahead, is your lack of direction. You also have little staying power. This means that if you are to achieve anything solid you need a lot of support and encouragement, particularly in your marriage and business partnerships. Yet you are certainly no fool, either intellectually or intuitively, and you love to learn. Indeed, academic qualifications are important to you. Because you can both understand and give a sympathetic ear to the problems of others, you are attracted to social work, counselling and psychiatry. However, your dislike of taking on too much responsibility means that you often miss out on the top jobs. You enjoy creative activities, such as drama, writing and music, and these take up much of your spare time. Your warm and sociable nature makes you popular, yet others find you hard to get to know because you tend to change your views and behaviour to suit the company. Thus, you are all things to all men. You have difficulty in starting new projects because you are a chronic procrastinator, which is another reason why you need a strong partner to give you a push. You dislike upsets and arguments, and you worry too much. Because you are poor at handling money, you often have problems with your finances. However, your intuitive abilities can give you good guidance – if you let them.

One of the biggest faults of a 7 ego is its tendency to be depressive and self-pitying. This is why its ideal complement is an id symbolized by 3, the number of the Sun at noon and of expansive Jupiter. But an id represented by 1, 5 or 9 can also stop a 7 ego from falling into the Slough of Despond too often. Yet this won't be the case if its partner is an id symbolized by 2, 4, 6 or 8, or by 7, for none of these can prevent it becoming depressed and miserable. In fact, they may worsen such tendencies.

An id symbolized by 7, however, is not a bad one to have, because 7, being the number of the Sun at its nadir, shows it to be well suited to its unconscious environment. Thus if you have a 7 id the deeper parts of your mind are not likely to contain much troublesome psychic material, so you should feel relatively at peace with yourself. You are very intuitive and you instinctively know how things will turn out. Indeed, with the right training you could make a competent medium or psychic. You are probably very interested in the occult and in mysterious happenings, and you may even like walking in cemeteries and attending funerals. Your dreams are vivid and colourful, and some of them are prophetic. You rather enjoy the ego-destabilizing effects of drink and drugs – even if the latter are only tranquillizers – and you need to use both cautiously. Your 7 id makes it easy for you to be alone, because you retreat into yourself, and you spend a lot of time day-dreaming. Your excellent understanding of human nature gives you a natural sympathy for others and the ability to give sensible advice. Yet because your conscience is poorly developed, you find it easy to fall down on your responsibilities. You rarely feel guilty!

If 7 is your name number you don't much like the outdoors, unless you are near water – by a lake, a river or the sea. You love visiting churches and cathedrals, indeed anywhere with religious connections, and places where the dead are buried. You prefer the company of women, especially after dark, your favourite time of the day. You like history and archaeology, stories about the sea, and anything strange or mysterious. In manner, you are truthful, God-fearing and reserved. Your lucky day of the week is Thursday; your lucky gemstones are the bloodstone, coral, the emerald and the sapphire; your lucky flower is the heliotrope; and your lucky colours are blue, mauve, purple and sea-green.

The Number 8

The number 8 is the last of the even single numbers, its smoothly curved shape suggesting balance and harmony. Its planet is Saturn, the faintest and the slowest-moving of the visible planets. In the solar cycle 8 represents the Sun's final placement before it rises to bring the new day. Thus it is, like 6 and 7, a number of the underworld.

But while 8 and Saturn are linked in a numerological sense, in myth Saturn is generally associated with 7, which as we have seen is one of the numbers of the Moon. To the Greeks, Cronus (or Saturn) was the seventh son of Uranus and Mother Earth, and was, as one of the Titans, the ruler of the seventh day, which is Saturday, the day of Saturn. Indeed, Saturn is the seventh planet.

We do know, however, that the ancient Greeks sacrificed to Selene, the Moon goddess, on the eighth day of each lunation, when the Moon enters its second phase. To them, the eighth day was sacred to the Moon.

More importantly, the god Saturn was originally both an agricultural deity and an aspect of the Moon, his lunar connections being made evident by his possession of an adamantine sickle, made for him by his mother, which is a symbol of the Moon. It is with the sickle that he castrates his father Uranus. The poet Hesiod describes what happened next:

> The genitals, cut off with adamant
> And thrown from land into the stormy sea,
> Were carried for a long time on the waves.
> White foam surrounded the immortal flesh,
> And in it grew a girl.

The girl is Aphrodite, the 'foam-born' goddess of love, who in reality is a third aspect of the Moon. Together, Aphrodite, Selene and Cronus – or, to give them their Latin names, Venus, Luna and Saturn – represent the Moon's three phases: New, Full and Old. This adds new meaning to the numbers 6, 7 and 8, the numbers of Venus, the Moon and Saturn, whose placement at the lowest point of the solar cycle reveals them to be not only numbers of the underworld, but of darkness and the night. Indeed, Venus, Luna and Saturn form the divine lunar triad, which is why their numbers, when added together, total 21 $(6 + 7 + 8 = 21)$, which in turn reduces to 3 $(2 + 1 = 3)$.

The myth of Saturn's seizure of heavenly power by castrating his father is symbolic of that distant period of human history when agriculture was fast supplanting hunting, and when life for many people was becoming much more stable, settled and peaceful. This golden 'age of Saturn', which was apparently initiated by women, who mastered agricultural production, brought about the eclipse of the old sky gods, symbolized by the castration of Uranus, and the worship in their place of Mother Earth and her celestial handmaiden, the Moon. The Greeks looked back longingly to this joyous and peaceful time, when people, so Hesiod tells us . . .

. . . lived with happy hearts
Untouched by work or sorrow . . .
. . . ungrudgingly, the fertile land
Gave up her fruits unasked. Happy to be
At peace, they lived with every want supplied.

The Old Moon's reaping of his father's genitals perhaps explains why Jehovah instructed Abraham that 'he that is eight days old shall be circumcized among you.' Circumcision exposes the hidden lunar glans of the penis, from whose centre emerges yellow urine and white fertilizing semen. Liquids have long been ruled by the Moon because it brings rain, and yellow and white are both lunar colours. The eighth day is wholly suitable for circumcision because the eighth day of the lunar cycle was, as we have seen, specially sacred to the Moon.

In keeping with Saturn's identification with the Old Moon, the number 8 symbolizes old age and those qualities of life that the later years bring forth, such as wisdom, self-control and patience. 8 is also the number of intuition and psychic ability, as well as being linked with money and business skills. Less happily, 8 represents gloom, despondency, regret and disillusion, and also obstacles, losses and difficulties.

8 is a potent factor in your life if you were born on the 8th, as it is, although less directly, if you started life on the 18th or the 28th. However, if your birthday falls on the latter date, you should appreciate that 28 is closely connected with the Moon, not only because 2 and 8 are both lunar numbers, but because the lunar cycle lasts for twenty-eight days. A birthday on the 28th makes you a Moon person: your life will wax and wane in keeping with the lunar rhythms, and you will feel peculiarly out-of-sorts at Full Moon. 8 is also important in the lives of those born in August, the eighth month. August was named for the Roman emperor Augustus to mark the month of his death. Coincidentally, Augustus was born in September when the Moon was lodged in the zodiac sign of Capricorn, whose planetary ruler is Saturn. Famous people with birthdays on the 8th include Sammy Davis Junior (8-12-1925), James Dean (8-2-1931), Dame Edith Evans (8-2-1888), Elvis Presley (8-1-1935), Robert Schumann (8-6-1810) and Harry S. Truman (8-5-1884).

If 8 is prominent in your birthdate you are tall and slim, with long limbs and somewhat starkly outlined bones. You have large teeth but because you don't smile very often they are seldom seen.

By nature you are retiring, introspective and unemotional. You are a loner, not simply because you enjoy your own company, but because you have difficulties in getting along with others. In fact, your personal relationships are always a bit fraught, due to your lack of a sense of humour and your somewhat acid tongue. You don't much care for the opposite sex and you may not marry until quite late in life, if at all. You have strong principles and a rather set way of looking at the world. You matured early and you will always seem old for your age. You dislike youthful high spirits and unruliness, as you do obvious displays of emotion. Because you have a good intuitive understanding of life, others find your thoughts and opinions valuable. However, although you are naturally conservative and law-abiding, you are quite capable of behaving aggressively if you feel you've been treated unfairly.

The colour of 8 is black, although any dark shade belongs to the number. The facial features of 8 people are strongly etched, their skin dry and sallow, and their hair coarse, straight and dark-coloured. The knees and knuckles are prominent. The direction of 8 is north-east, which is favourable for travel and residence for the 8 born. The best period for 8s occurs when Saturn passes through the zodiac sign of Libra, where it is exalted, the worst when Saturn is lodged in Aries, where it is debilitated. Because Saturn moves slowly through the sky, it stays in each sign for about two years. It ended its last transit of Libra in August, 1983 and it won't be back in the sign until early next century. Likewise, Saturn won't return to Aries until April 1996.

If your vowel number is 8, you have a stable and cautious ego personality, despite your occasional odd dreams and 'I know what's going to happen' hunches. You are conventional by instinct – some would say old-fashioned – and you dress and behave prudently and sensibly. Your chief personal fault is your relaxed attitude to cleanliness, which means that your finger nails and shirt collars are likely to be grubby. Sudden change alarms you, and indeed you can't stand people who are always changing their minds or who crave excitement. Your strategy of living is to plan ahead and work towards your goals slowly and carefully. You seldom expect immediate success. In fact, success for you is always viewed as a thing of the future, the pot of gold at the end of the rainbow which gives your life a point and a purpose. This is why many 8s feel decidedly unsettled when they reach their goals and why they immediately set new ones for themselves. You are patient and determined, traits which allow you to plod on determinedly for years. You are very careful with your money, to the extent that others regard you as being tight with it, and you're certainly not the sort who splashes money around. You like to have a sum of money salted away for emergencies, and you're very keen on investing anything extra, particularly in property or land. But what is most surprising about you in view of your carefully controlled emotions is your strong sex urge. Indeed, you don't like to waste any time in gratifying your sexual desires, thus sex is one of the few things that hurries you up.

Because 8 is the number of the Sun ascending from the underworld, your ego is ideally complemented by an id symbolized by 4, the number of the afternoon Sun. You are also well served by a 2 id, for such an id, like one symbolized by 4, has qualities that can alleviate your depressive tendencies. Less suitable is an id symbolized by 6 or 8, for both id types are too similar to your ego to be able to give it the necessary balance and lift. Similarly, an id represented by an odd number – 1, 3, 5, 7 or 9 – is unsatisfactory because it generates disruptive desires and changeable ideas which make it hard for you to feel at peace with yourself. This is especially true of a 7 id despite the lunar connections between 7 and 8. In fact, a 7 id is likely to weaken your confidence and increase your depression.

If you possess an 8 id you constantly sense that you must be careful and hold back, because such an id acts as a brake on your conscious self. In some respects this is advantageous to you, yet it may mean that you react too slowly when the circumstances call for fast action. Indeed, caution is your watchword and the slow, steady way always appeals to you more than the mad scramble. Waste, imprudence and poor organization upset you, and you feel ill-at-ease in situations where these are evident. You have great sympathy for those who want to preserve and conserve, and quite probably you belong to a conservation group yourself. You are loyal and dutiful, and your word is your bond. You hate behaving in ways that offend your sense of decency, no matter what the circumstances. But while your id seldom makes emotional demands on you, it is the source of your strong sex urge. How this is expressed depends, of course, on your ego type, but if it is adequately controlled and directed it can be a powerful aid, giving you tremendous energy and drive. Uncontrolled, it may bring you much distress and many problems. You also have trouble in forgiving and forgetting, which means you tend to waste too much time in righting old wrongs. Others find you cool and laid-back and they sense, no matter what your ego type, that you keep things from them.

If 8 is your name number you are happiest outdoors at places that are wooded or mountainous, or that are near lakes and rivers. You prefer foods that grow beneath the earth, like potatoes, or those that are dark in colour, like prunes. You also enjoy eating meat and fish and all food and drink that has been matured for a long time. In particular, you like sharp tastes. Your favourite season of the year is winter, and you are strongly attracted to old people, rubbish tips, unsavoury places like brothels and low-class nightclubs, and areas of town frequented by workers, rough-necks and vagabonds. You have a talent for languages and a love of anything to do with the soil. Your lucky day of the week is Saturday; your lucky gemstones are the garnet, the black opal and the tourmaline; your lucky flowers are the nightshade, the rose and the thistle; and your lucky colours are black, grey and indigo.

The Number 9

The number 9 is the last single odd number as well as being the last single number. In the solar cycle it corresponds to the rising Sun, specifically to that half of the Sun which is still below the horizon. Its planet is Mars, the red planet, who in mythology was the god of war.

In ancient times 9 was also linked with the Moon. We have already seen how the Moon's three phases – New, Full and Old – were represented by a trio of deities, such as Venus, Luna and Saturn. In time each god or goddess of the Moon's three phases similarly became represented by a triad, thereby increasing the number of lunar deities to nine.

9 is the number of birth and new life because the period of human gestation is nine months. Indeed, the mystery of birth and the mechanics of addition give 9 its secret meaning: it is the number of endings but also of beginnings. Gestation takes nine months and terminates with the birth of the child, while 9 itself is followed by 10, which reduces to 1 ($1 + 0 = 1$) to start a new sequence. Thus 9 is the final stage of a continually repeated series.

Greek mythology provides many examples of 9 representing the end of one activity and the start of another. Typically, some significant event occurs on the ninth day, in the ninth month or in the ninth year.

For instance, when Phyllis, the lover of Acamas, heard that

Troy had fallen she went each night to the sea-shore to watch for his ship. When it failed to appear on her ninth visit she died of grief and was transformed into an almond tree. Again, Deucalion and Pyrrha, the Greek survivors of the flood, floated helplessly in their ark for nine days before it came to rest on Mount Parnassus, while Britomartis, the daughter, like Artemis, of Leto and thus a lunar deity, was chased by Minos for nine months before eluding capture by throwing herself into the sea.

The ninth year was especially important to the Greeks because nine years comprised the Great Year of one hundred lunations, and because childhood ended for the Greeks at age nine.

Thus the god Hephaistos, having been flung from Olympus at birth by his mother Hera, is restored by her to the sacred mountain in his ninth year. And it was at the age of nine that the twins Otus and Ephialtes, both of whom stood nine fathoms tall and measured nine cubits across, attempted to scale Mount Olympus by piling Mount Pelion on Mount Ossa. Similarly, it was every ninth year that the Athenians were obliged to send a tribute of seven youths and seven maidens to Crete as an offering for the Minotaur.

9 is therefore the number of both completion and incipient regeneration, and hence of wisdom and the expert as well as ignorance and the novice, of sense and nonsense, of caution and imprudence, of virtue and licence, and of the follower and the leader. In these respects it accords with the mythological nature of the god Mars, who while being strong, fearless and skilled in warfare, was also impetuous, impatient and rash, characteristics that led to his defeat in battle on more than one occasion.

If you were born on the 9th of any month, 9 is an important influence in your life. This is also true, albeit to a lesser extent, if you were born on the 19th or the 29th. 9 is likewise important in the lives of those born in September, the ninth month, although it was originally the seventh month of the year (*Septem* is Latin for 'seven'). The Romans held games called the *Ludi Romani* in September, which ran from the 5th to the 19th of the month. Famous people with birthdays on the 9th include Kirk Douglas (9-12-1916), Edward Heath (9-7-1916), John Lennon (9-10-1940), Richard Nixon (9-1-1913), Donny Osmond (9-12-1957) and Peter the Great of Russia (9-5-1672).

Should 9 be well represented in your birthdate you are probably of average height with a strong, muscular body. If you are a man you are likely to have a moustache or a beard, or both, and if you are woman you may be troubled with unwanted facial or body hair. Also, you probably possess a mark, such as a prominent mole, birthmark or scar, on your head or face. You are an outgoing, confident type with a lot of energy, courage and panache. Unfortunately, you like your own way and you can't stand being frustrated. If you are, you quickly lose your cool. Your impatience makes you accident-prone and thus a danger to both yourself and others. Because you like change, excitement and adventure, you are always ready to accept new ideas and new challenges. Yet you all too frequently start new schemes without adequate planning or thought, with the result that they often come to grief. Similarly, you just as quickly lose interest, for you are by nature a starter rather than a finisher. This is why others are wary of asking you for help because they know you cannot be relied upon.

9 is the number of red and of all roseate shades. 9 people usually have ruddy faces and curly red, brown or black hair. Their voices are loud and rather coarse and their movements are clumsy. The direction of 9, like that of 1, is east, which is fortunate for travel and residence for both 1s and 9s. The best period for 9 people occurs when Mars passes through Capricorn, where it is exalted, their worse when Mars transits Cancer, where it is debilitated. Mars generally stays for about five weeks in each of the signs, although this can be considerably lengthened by its retrogradation. Mars next travels through Cancer between 21 May and 6 July 1987 and through Capricorn between 23 February 1988 and 6 April 1988.

If you have a 9 vowel number, which is symbolic of your ego, you possess an excitable, hot-blooded personality, which makes you both extroverted and pushy. You like to be noticed and for this reason you tend to favour brash, eye-catching clothes. Because you see things in black-and-white terms, you're either for or against in your attitudes, there being no in-between for you. You like to deal with your problems promptly and decisively, which is why you will resort to violence if all else fails. You are touchy about how others treat you, because you want and expect their deference and admiration. For this reason you have constant arguments with your friends, simply to maintain your place in the pecking order. But while you are selfish and somewhat arrogant, you more than make up for those faults with your enthusiasm and generosity. If you like someone you'll go overboard in supporting him or her, thus you make a powerful and stimulating ally. Also, because you like facing challenges and opposing those in authority, you are always ready to help someone in trouble, especially if this means you have to take on those in government or the police. Because you are open and forthright, you don't pull any punches when it comes to saying what you think. Thus you're not a hypocrite or a dissembler. You're just as open with your heart, which you lose very easily. In fact, you love the company of the opposite sex. But unfortunately, although you are always open to new ideas and experiences – to the extent that you know more about life than most – your impatience and impulsiveness often gets in the way of your wisdom and developed caution. In this respect you are the eternal optimist.

Because 9 is the number of the rising Sun, you are best served by an id symbolized by 5, the number of the setting Sun. But an id symbolized by 3 or 7 is also suitable for you, as both types complement your conscious self. This is not the case if your id is symbolized by 1, because it will be very similar to your ego in character, or by 9 itself. Your ego type is the exception where even-numbered ids are concerned, for such ids reduce your tendency to run out of control. However, they may make you somewhat manic-depressive.

If you have a 9 id you have a turbulent inner life, and your unconscious is likely to be the source of all manner of desires, urges and images that not only make it hard for you to relax but which may upset you. You probably feel dissatisfied with what you have achieved and are constantly trying to do better. But, of course, your dissatisfaction depends on your ego type, although if you're the sort of person who likes to think ahead and plan your moves, your 9 id will naturally encourage you to take short-cuts and to run instead of walk. Such advice isn't always wrong, however, and for this reason you are well advised to pay attention to your dreams and hunches, which can guide you as to how you should proceed. Because you are inquisitive and curious you need to work in a field that satisfies your desire to know. Your sexual urge is strong and you spend quite a lot of time thinking about sex. You fall in love quickly, but not always wisely. You are not very constant in your affections, which may provoke strong guilt feelings if your ego nature believes in loyalty and fair play. You hate to be enclosed, thus you can't stand small rooms, closed doors and windows, or lifts. Indeed, any form of restriction makes you uncomfortable.

If 9 is your name number you like being in the country during the day and in town at night. You enjoy noise, colour, activity and crowds – and you can't resist watching a military display. You are fond of sports and games, pungent tastes, gold or copper jewellery and ornaments, warm temperatures, fire and fireworks, your brothers, horses and a good laugh. Your lucky day of the week is Tuesday; your lucky gemstones are the diamond and the ruby; your lucky flowers are the geranium, the gorse, the thistle and the wild rose; and your lucky colours are bright green, pink, red and russet.

3

Numbers and Inner Harmony

The two areas of the mind, the ego and the id, together reflect the polarity of nature. The ego or conscious is the part of the mind that is self-aware, the part with which we think and reflect. The id or unconscious is the part of the mind that is hidden, wherein memories, feelings and emotions are kept essentially locked away. The ego corresponds to the positive pole – to light openness and freedom – and the id to the negative pole, that is, to darkness, confinement and restriction.

Yet there is a constant two-way interaction between the ego and the id. During the day the active ego sends all its sense impressions and thoughts to the id, where they are stored as memory. At night, when the ego is relatively quiescent, the id communicates with it symbolically through dreams. This is why Freud called dreams the 'royal road to the unconscious'.

For a person to be happy with himself and with the world harmony must exist between his ego and id. Such harmony only occurs when the id is free of troublesome feelings or when the ego ceases to be bothered by them. Disharmony thus results from tensions between the ego and the id, to the extent that meaningful interaction between them has ceased, so that they are in essence separate poles instead of being two sides of the same coin.

As we have seen, a person's ego is represented by the vowel value of his name, and his id by the consonant value. This naturally implies that the name itself symbolizes the whole man or woman.

There is nothing far-fetched about this. After all, if I ask you who you are, you will reply, 'I am John Smith', or whatever. Your name, to all intents and purposes, is you. It stands for all that you are. Indeed, there is evidence which suggests that a name is more than just a symbol, but rather a shaping force. It has been shown, for example, that those with impressive or remarkable names

often become impressive or remarkable people while those with
ordinary names tend to stay ordinary. But there is nothing new in
the idea that names have power. Down the ages countless statesmen,
politicians, artists, actors and entertainers have transformed themselves by taking pseudonyms, and without their adopted names we
would probably never have heard of Caligula, N. Lenin, Joseph
Stalin, Leon Trotsky, Mark Twain, George Eliot, George Sand,
Samuel Goldwyn, George Orwell, Ginger Rogers, Tony Curtis,
Kirk Douglas, Ringo Starr, Cliff Richard, Alvin Stardust and
Engelbert Humperdinck, to name but a few.

But more importantly, we can, by using our name's vowel and
consonant values, determine how well each relates to the other
and thus the degree of compatibility that exists between our ego
and id.

This numerological way of discovering how balanced we are
psychically also works practically in the other direction. For if we
find that our ego and id types are incompatible, we can, by
changing our names, alter either our ego or id numbers, or both,
and thereby bring about a healthy change in our psyche. Such a
change can and will bring about quite amazing results, as many
thousands of people have discovered, while at the same time
having the added advantage of being free, which qualified
psychiatric help is most certainly not.

Of course, the idea of changing your name might sound
daunting to you. But then, you would be very unusual if it didn't
because your name is you. Yet such a change is a small price to pay
for becoming a happier and better adjusted person. And anyhow,
if you want to create a new you, there's no reason why the new you
shouldn't have a new name.

Fortunately, however, a name change doesn't have to be radical
and quite possibly you can achieve an improved vowel/consonant
relationship by tinkering with your given names. Consider, for
example, the case of a man named John Peter Jones, who grew up
calling himself John Jones and who wasn't at all happy. Now John
Jones has a vowel number of 8 and a consonant number of 3:

$$\text{JOHN JONES}$$
$$6 \qquad 6 \quad 5 \; = 17 = 8$$

$$\text{JOHN JONES}$$
$$1 \; 8\,5\,1 \quad 5 \; 1 = 21 = 3$$

John Jones thus has an 8 ego type and a 3 id type, which as we know, are incompatible, one being even numbered and one odd numbered.

But John Peter Jones has a remedy at hand by dropping his first Christian name, John, in favour of his second, Peter. Peter Jones gives him a 3 vowel number and a 7 consonant number:

PETER JONES
5 5 6 5 = 21 = 3

PETER JONES
7 2 9 1 5 1 = 25 = 7

A 3 ego and a 7 id are a perfect match because not only are they both odd numbered, but their numbers are opposites. Moreover, 3 is a natural ego number because it is the number of the Sun at midday, while 7 is a natural id number because it is the number of the Sun at its nadir. Furthermore, John Jones had a 3 id. By becoming Peter Jones he is able to release his troublesome id contents into his ego, his new id thereby becoming transformed into a heathier 7 type.

The name Peter Jones has another advantage, for Peter, in common with many other first names, is often shortened – to Pete. But fortunately, the name Pete Jones gives exactly the same vowel/consonant number values as Peter Jones:

PETE JONES
5 5 6 5 = 21 = 3

PETE JONES
7 2 1 5 1 = 16 = 7

Thus Peter Jones, in terms of producing a psychologically well-adjusted person, is a perfect name.

Should it be necessary, you may also be able to improve your psychological balance just as easily, if not by using one of your other Christian names in full, then perhaps by shortening it, in the manner that Maureen can be abbreviated to Mo, Elizabeth to Liz, Reginald to Reg, Herbert to Herb or Bert, and so on. If not, you will have to adopt an entirely new Christian name to give you the number balance that you require.

It is normal, of course, for women to take a new surname when they marry and such a change either gives them improved vowel/consonant number values or worse ones. Only rarely do their vowel and consonant numbers stay the same. These changes reflect the changes in their lives that the married state brings about, improved vowel/consonant number values usually indicating a happy marriage and worsened vowel/consonant number values the reverse. It therefore follows that if an unhappily married woman alters her name in the manner described above to give herself better vowel/consonant number values, the improvement in her mental state that this will cause will enable her to function more effectively, which may in turn make her marriage happier.

Finally, it remains to be said that the profound mental changes that can be brought about by a change of name do not happen overnight. They take time, often quite a long time. How long? Well, about as long as it took Peter Jones to feel that he really is Peter Jones, and not John Jones, that is, for as long as it takes your new name to sink totally into your mind, so that it, and not your old name, is you.

PART TWO:
NUMBERS AND THE FUTURE

4

NUMBERS AND DESTINY

Our existence, it has been said, has only two certainties: one, nothing remains the same; two, life ends in death. Everything else is a guess, a perhaps and a maybe.

But not quite. There are ways of lifting Fortuna's veils and taking a peek at what lies ahead, and some of these – like astrology, palmistry and the interpretation of omens – have been used for millennia. Yet despite their age and accuracy, such methods have one major drawback: they require expert knowledge, knowledge that most people nowadays are too busy to acquire for themselves.

Fortunately, however, numerology gives anyone the power to understand the course of his or her life, in a way that is both easy to use and mathematically precise.

The most important number in this respect is the birth or destiny number. You will remember that this is obtained by adding together the numbers of one's birthdate and reducing the result to a single number.

Again, consider the birthdate 7 April 1963. This reduces to 3, the birth number:

$$7 + 4 + 1 + 9 + 6 + 3 = 30$$
$$3 + 0 = 3$$

If you haven't already done so, now is the time to calculate your own birth number.

Using your birth number, you can determine those periods of your life which are generally favourable, those which are generally unfavourable, and those which are neutral, that is, which bring good and bad in roughly equal amounts.

The system we shall use to do this is based on the seven planets of traditional astrology and the numbers associated with them. It is a very accurate method of elucidating future trends, as the examples discussed demonstrate, and should be considered carefully.

The first important fact to appreciate is that each stage of your life – or, for that matter, anyone's life – is governed by one of the planets. The order in which they govern is determined by their apparent distance from the earth. The Moon, for example, rules us at birth because it is closest to us: then comes Mercury, Venus, the Sun, Mars, Jupiter and Saturn. This order does not entirely agree with the discoveries of modern astronomy, yet it is surprisingly close.

The length of each planetary period derives from the number linked with the governing planet, which represents the same number of years. Thus because the number linked with Mars is 9, the period governed by Mars lasts for nine years.

The Moon is associated with two numbers, 2 and 7. At birth the first of these is operative, which means that the first two years of anyone's life are ruled by the Moon.

The planet Mercury is linked with 5, hence the next five years of life are ruled by Mercury.

Similarly, the next six years are ruled by Venus, whose number is 6. But because the Sun, like the Moon, is linked with two numbers, 1 and 4, and because 1 is initially operative, only the succeeding year is governed by the Sun. The following nine years are ruled by Mars (9), the next three by Jupiter (3), and the next eight by Saturn (8). This takes us up to our 34th birthday.

From this age the cycle of planets repeats itself, except that instead of the Moon ruling the following two years it governs the next seven, because 7 is the second of its two numbers. Likewise, the Sun rules four years instead of only one. This second planetary cycle takes us to our 76th birthday. From then on the first cycle operates again, with the Moon ruling the next two years, so taking us to age 110 which is the greatest age that anyone can realistically hope to live to. (The oldest authenticated age to which anyone has ever lived is 113 years, 124 days, which was achieved by the French-Canadian bootmaker Pierre Joubert.)

These three complete planetary cycles correspond to the three lengths of life referred to by Indian astrologers: *Alpayu* or short life (birth to age 32), *Madhyayu* or medium life (age 32 to age 75), and *Purnayu* or full life (age 75 to 120). The Indians believe that the full human lifespan is 120, which accords with Genesis 5:3 – 'And the Lord said, My spirit shall not always strive with man, for that he also is flesh: yet his days shall be an hundred and twenty years.'

The table below shows the planetary periods of human life and their length:

	Planet	Number	Age
First Cycle	Moon	2	0-2
	Mercury	5	2-7
	Venus	6	7-13
	Sun	1	13-14
	Mars	9	14-23
	Jupiter	3	23-26
	Saturn	8	26-34
Second Cycle	Moon	7	34-41
	Mercury	5	41-46
	Venus	6	46-52
	Sun	4	52-56
	Mars	9	56-65
	Jupiter	3	65-68
	Saturn	8	68-76
Third Cycle	Moon	2	76-78
	Mercury	5	78-83
	Venus	6	83-89
	Sun	1	89-90
	Mars	9	90-99
	Jupiter	3	99-102
	Saturn	8	102-110

This table will enable you to discover which planetary period you are currently in. Obviously, if you are 24 years old you are under the rulership of Jupiter, if 70 years old you are under the rulership of Saturn.

The first point of importance about these planetary periods is that each will treat you in a manner determined by your birth number. Some will be favourable, some unfavourable and some neutral. Thus a continuous, yet consistent cycle of change threads its way through your life, the key to which is provided by your birth number.

There are two types of favourable period: the good or single positive (+) and the very good or double positive (++). Likewise, there are two types of unfavourable period, the bad or single negative (−) and the very bad or double negative (− −). By contrast, there is only one type of neutral period (0). These periods correspond to the positive, negative and neutral points of the solar cycle, which are illustrated below:

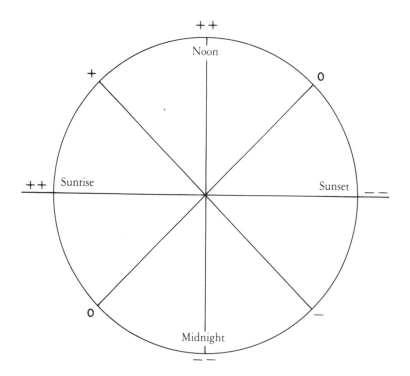

To determine the nature of your own life periods, you must put your birth number at the double positive (++) sunrise position and place the remaining numbers in sequence around the circle. The numbers and the periods they and their planets rule all take the positive, negative and neutral qualities of the points where they fall. The diagram at the top of the next page shows how the sequence would look if your birth number is 7.

This tells us that the most favourable or double positive periods (++) are linked with 7, 1 and 9 and the favourable or single positive periods (+) with 8, that the most unfavourable or double negative periods (--) are linked with 3 and 5 and the unfavourable or single negative periods (-) with 4, and that the neutral periods are linked with 2 and 6. The table on page 66 shows how these would appear in your life.

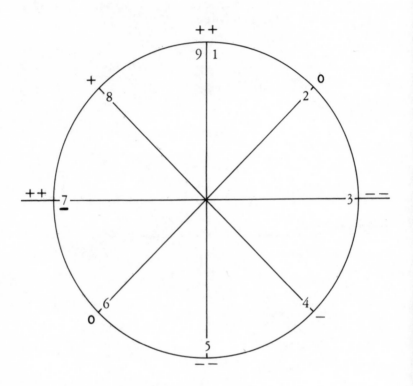

Planet	Number	Age	Nature
Moon	2	0-2	0
Mercury	5	2-7	- -
Venus	6	7-13	0
Sun	1	13-14	++
Mars	9	14-23	++
Jupiter	3	23-26	- -
Saturn	8	26-34	+
Moon	7	34-41	++
Mercury	5	41-46	- -
Venus	6	46-52	0
Sun	4	52-56	-
Mars	9	56-65	++
Jupiter	3	65-68	- -
Saturn	8	68-76	+	etc.

This means that up until the age of 76 your best life periods would lie between the ages of 13 and 14 (1), 14 and 23 (9), 34 and 41 (7) and 56 and 65 (9). Conversely, your most difficult periods would lie between the ages of 2 and 7 (5), 23 and 26 (3), 41 and 46 (5) and 65 and 68 (3). The other periods would all fall somewhere between these two extremes, being either single positive, single negative or neutral.

The nature of the life periods are obviously different for those with different birth numbers, with the exception of those with a birth number of either 1 or 9, who, because their birth numbers occupy the same point in the solar cycle, share life periods having the same nature.

The following solar wheel shows the positive, negative and neutral number points of someone having a 4 birth number:

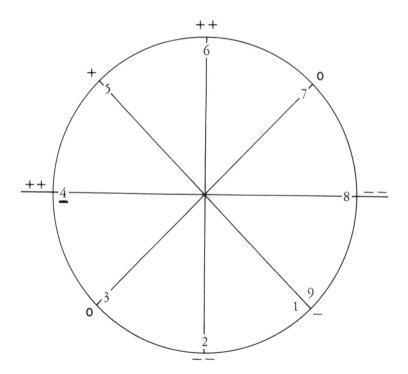

For this person the double positive periods (++) lie between the ages of 7 and 13 (6), 46 and 52 (6) and 51 and 56 (4), at least up until the age of 76. The double negative periods lie between birth and the age of 2 (2), 26 and 34 (8) and 68 and 76 (8).

The table below shows the nature of the life periods for each of the nine birth number types:

Planet	Age	Birth Number								
		1	2	3	4	5	6	7	8	9
Moon (2)	0-2	+	++	0	- -	-	- -	0	++	+
Mercury (5)	2-7	- -	0	++	+	++	0	- -	-	- -
Venus (6)	7-13	-	- -	0	++	+	++	0	- -	-
Sun (1)	13-14	++	0	- -	-	- -	0	++	+	++
Mars (9)	14-23	++	0	- -	-	- -	0	++	+	++
Jupiter (3)	23-26	++	+	++	0	- -	-	- -	0	++
Saturn (8)	26-34	0	- -	-	- -	0	++	+	++	0
Moon (7)	34-41	- -	-	- -	0	++	+	++	0	- -
Mercury (5)	41-46	- -	0	++	+	++	0	- -	-	- -
Venus (6)	46-52	-	- -	0	++	+	++	0	- -	-
Sun (4)	52-56	0	++	+	++	0	- -	-	- -	0
Mars (9)	56-65	++	0	- -	-	- -	0	++	+	++
Jupiter (3)	65-68	++	+	++	0	- -	-	- -	0	++
Saturn (8)	68-76	0	- -	-	- -	0	++	+	++	0
Moon (2)	76-78	+	++	0	- -	-	- -	0	++	+
Mercury (5)	78-83	- -	0	++	+	++	0	- -	-	- -
Venus (6)	83-89	-	- -	0	++	+	++	0	- -	-
Sun (1)	89-90	++	0	- -	-	- -	0	++	+	++

By looking down the column under your birth number you can now see which life periods (or ages) will be good for you, which bad and which neutral. The good periods are the ones which have the greatest potential for happiness and success, when things tend to fall into place for you and when life is generally easier. The bad periods – especially the ones that are double negative (– –) – are those which throw up the biggest problems and difficulties, when life tends to be less enjoyable and more fraught. In particular, these are more likely to produce illness, accidents and death, although the worst does not by any means always happen in a double negative period. For just as a double positive period has the most potential for good, so the double negative period has the most potential for bad. If you are wise you will take maximum advantage of the former – to study, to start a business, to marry –

while proceeding cautiously and prudently during the latter. In this way you can accentuate the good and minimize the bad.

An examination of the lives of the famous reveals that most reached the pinnacle of their successes during a double positive period, and that their major difficulties, sometimes even their deaths, happened in a double negative period. A few examples will demonstrate this.

Elvis Presley, nicknamed 'the Pelvis', burst onto the music scene in the mid-1950s, to quickly become the most dynamic singing star the world has ever seen. He almost single-handedly launched rock 'n' roll, and his driving singing style, sexy movements and outrageous clothes were widely admired and imitated.

But although Elvis Presley was destined to become very rich and famous, he was born into humble circumstances on 8 January 1935, the son of Vernon and Gladys Presley, both poor, working-class whites.

Elvis's birthdate gave him a 9 birth number:

$$8 + 1 + 1 + 9 + 3 + 5 = 27$$
$$2 + 7 = 9$$

As can be seen from the above table, the first two years of Elvis Presley's life were single positive ones; the following eleven years, however, weren't nearly so good. His five-year Mercury period from age 2 to 7 was double negative and his six-year Venus period from the age of 7 to 13 was single negative. His family's fortunes remained at a low ebb at this time, both parents working at a succession of low-paid jobs, their joint income too low to enable them to move from the two-room wood shack where Elvis had been born. Their nadir happened during Elvis's five-year Mercury period, when father Vernon was sent to gaol for trying to cash a forged cheque.

Elvis started a double positive (++) Sun period on his 13th birthday and that year – 1948 – things started to change for the better. The Presley family moved to Memphis, a city of some size and a growing music centre, and it wasn't long before they were housed in a large and quite pleasant apartment at Lauderdale Court. Elvis was sent to Humes High School and on graduating in 1952 he found himself a job as a truck-driver, while making tentative efforts to launch a singing career.

Elvis left school and started work during his double positive Mars period, which began for him at the age of 14 and continued until his 23rd birthday (1949-58). It was during this period that he leapt to stardom. In 1954 he had gained the stage at Overton Park Shell in Memphis, making up part of a local music show. In 1955, 'That's All Right, Mama' was released, making him a local celebrity. Then in 1956 'Heartbreak Hotel' became a national hit, and Elvis's appearance on the Ed Sullivan show sent him rocketing into orbit. From that moment on his records consistently topped the charts and teenagers everywhere went wild for him.

The Mars period ended on his birthday in 1958. It was followed, however, by another double positive period, one which lasted for three years and was ruled by the planet Jupiter (1958-61).

Apart from being the planet of growth and increase, Jupiter governs religion, education and travel. Thus it was perhaps not surprising that Elvis was inducted into the Army in March 1958 and was soon afterwards posted to Germany. But the stunned world had no reason to worry about his fortunes. He remained as popular as ever and his records continued to sell like hotcakes.

Elvis's two-year Army stint ended in March 1960, when he returned to America. He immediately made some new records, employing both a different style and a different band. Two of these records – 'It's Now or Never' and 'Are You Lonesome Tonight?' – became his biggest sellers.

Elvis Presley's decline as a singing star can be dated to 1961, when he started an eight-year neutral period ruled by Saturn (1961-9). It was during this period that he stopped making live appearances and instead concentrated on becoming a film-star. He was to appear in a total of thirty-three films, the majority of which were candy floss epics, characterized by poor acting, poor plots and poor songs. Never again was Elvis Presley to be the raunchy rocker of his pre-Army days.

In 1967 he married Priscilla Beaulieu, and their daughter Lisa was born on 1 February 1968 – exactly nine months to the day after their marriage. Like her father, Lisa Presley has a 9 birth number.

The eight-year neutral period, which was more than a little disappointing to Elvis's fans, ended on the singers birthday in 1969. It was followed by two double negative periods, the first lasting seven years and ruled by the Moon (1969-76), the second lasting five years and ruled by Mercury (1976-81). These periods were to be the most difficult and tragic of Elvis's life, notwithstanding the fact that he began touring again. For he had become a drug addict, a habit begun in his neutral period but which became far more serious in 1969. After his divorce from Priscilla in 1973, a break-up that affected him deeply, he went into a steady decline, his health rapidly worsening: he suffered from a chronic weight problem, diabetes, digestive disorders, glaucoma and heart irregularities, all of which were adversely affected by his heavy drug-taking.

Elvis Presley died suddenly in his bathroom on 16 August 1977, about eighteen months after the start of his second double negative period.

Of course, Elvis Presley is a special case and his life should not be regarded as a mirror for those with a 9 birth number. Few people with this birth number will experience either the huge success or the steep decline and early death of Elvis Presley. Yet they will find that the same double positive periods offer them their greatest advantages and the same double negative periods their biggest difficulties.

By way of contrast, we will next consider the life of Adolf Hitler, the German dictator and founder of Nazism.

Hitler was born in Braunau-am-Inn, Austria, on 20 April 1889. He therefore had a birth number of 5:

$$2 + 0 + 4 + 1 + 8 + 8 + 9 = 32$$
$$3 + 2 = 5$$

Despite the fact that the first two years of his life were single negative (1889-91), he survived them, which was more than his two brothers had done, and the close relationship he enjoyed with his mother doubtless helped make the following five years (1891-6) as positive as they were. He began a single positive period on his 7th birthday in 1896, and this lasted until his 13th birthday in 1902, when he began three consecutive double negative periods. The first, ruled by the Sun, lasted for one year (1902-3). The second, ruled by Mars, ran for nine years (1903-12), and the third, ruled by Jupiter, lasted for three years (1912-15). This long and difficult period had a decisive psychological effect on Hitler, for it was during this time that he acquired his deep hatred of Jews and of liberal values and developed his admiration for Germany.

Hitler's father Alois died in 1903, at the start of young Adolf's double negative Mars period. He left school in 1905 without the normal leaving certificate, one of his masters describing him as being 'notoriously cantankerous, wilful, arrogant and bad-tempered', and spent the next two years drifting around Linz, where he and his sick mother Klara were then living. In 1907 he went to Vienna, where he twice unsuccessfully tried to gain a place at the Academy of Fine Arts. For the next three years he lived in a men's hostel and supported himself by doing odd jobs. He said later, 'Vienna was a hard school for me, but it taught me the most profound lessons of my life.'

In 1913, during the three-year double negative Jupiter period, Hitler moved to Munich in German Bavaria. The following year the First World War broke out and he immediately volunteered for active service. He was in uniform throughout the war, and he was wounded twice and twice decorated with the Iron Cross. He never rose, however, above the rank of corporal.

Hitler began a neutral period on his 26th birthday in 1915 and it was after this date that he won the decorations mentioned above. Certainly the quality of his life improved. At the end of the war he stayed on in the Army, was made an education officer and was sent to Munich to counter Communist propaganda and to observe the activities of small political groups.

In September 1919 he attended a meeting of the German Workers' Party and was immediately attracted by its policies. He joined it and became, oddly enough, its fifty-fifth member, receiving a membership card numbered 555. He rose quickly through its ranks, helped swell its membership with his rousing speeches, and on 24 February 1920 announced its anti-Semitic, pro-Aryan racial policies to a crowd of 2,000 at the Hofbrauhous beer cellar in Munich. The party's name was augmented to the National Socialist German Workers' Party – or Nazi Party, for short – and the swastika and the raised arm salute were adopted as its symbols. The following year Adolf Hitler became its leader.

But things did not go entirely Hitler's way during this neutral period. He injudiciously proclaimed a revolution in 1923, but his 'march on Berlin' was broken up by the police, who shot and killed sixteen of his followers. For this debacle Hitler was sent to gaol for nine months.

Hitler's birthday in 1923 saw the end of the eight-year neutral period which had governed his life since 1915 and the start of a double positive period. In fact, two double positive periods ran consecutively for him, the first a seven-year period ruled by the Negative Moon (1923-30), the second a five-year period ruled by Mercury (1930-35). It was during this long twelve-year period that Adolf Hitler rose to supreme power in Germany, for despite the Nazis' defeat in the 1928 elections, the continuing economic downswing ensured that they more than recouped their losses in the elections of 1930, when they became the second largest political party in Germany. Chancellor Franz von Papen called another election in 1932, in the hope of factionalizing the Nazis, but their share of the Reichstag seats again increased. The following year, after von Papen had been forced to resign, Adolf Hitler was made Chancellor. In 1934 Hitler eliminated his rivals in the Nazi Party and on Hindenberg's death in the August of that year he assumed the title of President. He had become the Führer, the leader.

Hitler began a single positive period on his birthday in 1935 which lasted for six years (1935-41). During this period he successfully reduced German unemployment and began to put his plans for German reunification, which he had described in *Mein Kampf*, into action. He stripped German Jews of their citizenship and initiated the 'Final Solution'. In 1936 he invaded the Rhineland and in 1938 he annexed Austria. In September 1938 he signed the Munich Agreement with Neville Chamberlain, Daladier and Mussolini. The following year he annexed Bohemia and Morovia, thereafter signing the Pact of Steel with Italy on 22 May and, to everybody's amazement, a non-aggression treaty with Russia on 23 August. On 1 September 1939 Hitler ordered his troops into Poland, to which Britain and France responded by declaring war on Germany on 3 September. The Second World War had begun.

The success of the German forces continued, however, due largely to the unpreparedness of the Allies. Hitler's Stormtroops quickly overran Denmark and Norway, then France, Belgium, Holland and Luxemburg. Yet the planned invasion of Britain was not mounted, because the Luftwaffe were defeated by the RAF in the Battle of Britain. It was this reverse that persuaded Hitler to go ahead with his plans for the invasion of Russia. Operation Barbarossa was launched on 22 June 1941, just two months after the start of the four-year neutral period which governed Hitler's life until 1945. The invasion of Russia proceeded far more quickly and successfully than Hitler expected, and it seemed likely that the German Army would reach Moscow by Christmas 1941. But there was a sudden stiffening of Russian resolve, which had been badly shaken by the speed and ferocity of the German attack, and the rate of the Wermacht's advance was slowed. This marked, although Hitler did not know it at the time, the beginning of the end for the Third Reich. Hitler's days were numbered.

It is unnecessary to chart the remaining course of the war – the retreat from Moscow, the entry into the conflict of the United States, the Allied victories – except to remark that the noose kept tightening around Germany's neck. By April 1945 the Russians had surrounded Berlin, trapping the Führer in his underground bunker. On 20 April Hitler celebrated his 56th birthday, which also marked the start of a double negative period ruled by Mars. Nine days later he married his mistress Eva Braun. The following day – 30 April 1945 – he shot himself. Not long afterwards the war ended and Europe began picking up the pieces. The nightmare was over.

Adolf Hitler's life demonstrates, like that of Elvis Presley's, that it is the double positive periods which offer the greatest potential for advancement. The key double positive period in this respect is the one ruled by the planet associated with one's birth number. Elvis Presley (birth number 9) became internationally famous as a singer during the nine-year Mars period that governed his life between the ages of 13 and 23, and Adolf Hitler (birth number 5) became dictator of Germany during the five-year Mercury period that governed him between the ages of 41 and 46. But such a period is, however, a moment of time which has to be siezed: it does not automatically confer its blessings upon those living through it. Both Elvis Presley and Adolf Hitler had set their goals and were working towards them when their moment came. They made their right time work for them.

Similarly, the most hazardous double negative period is the one linked with the number that lies opposite one's birth number in the solar cycle. For example, 5 is the number lying opposite 9 in the solar cycle and it was during the five-year Mercury period that ruled his life between ages 41 and 46 that Elvis Presley died (at age 42). Likewise, 1 and 9 are the numbers that lie opposite 5 in the solar cycle and it was during the nine-year Mars period that ruled his life between the ages of 56 and 65 that Adolf Hitler died (at 56). Of course, death does not always happen during such a period, but one is always at risk.

Finally, let us take a brief look at the career of Margaret Thatcher, the Prime Minister of Britain.

Margaret Hilda Thatcher was born on 13 October 1925. She thus has a 4 birth number:

$$1 + 3 + 1 + 0 + 1 + 9 + 2 + 5 = 22$$
$$2 + 2 = 4$$

Mrs Thatcher spent her childhood in the town of her birth – Grantham, in Lincolnshire – and she has often said how happy it was and how she draws strength from the values it taught her. It is therefore not surprising to find that she enjoyed a five-year single positive period between the ages of 2 and 7 (1927-32), which was followed by a six-year double positive period between the ages of 7 and 13 (1932-8). She then began a long and less fortunate period which ran from her 13th birthday to her 41st. This consisted of (1) two consecutive single negative periods, the first lasting a year (1938-9), the second nine years (1939-48), during the latter part of which she attended Oxford University and gained a degree in Chemistry, (2) a three-year neutral period (1948-51) when she worked as a research chemist and began to study law, (3) an eight-year double negative period (1951-9), during which she completed her law studies, being called to the Bar in 1953, and (4) another neutral period which lasted for seven years (1959-66). She married her husband Denis when she was 25, just before she began the double negative period, and she entered Parliament in 1959, shortly after the double negative period ended.

Although we know little about Mrs Thatcher's private life and inner feelings between 1938 and 1966, the fact that she changed her career three times – from research chemist to lawyer to politician – while coping with being a wife and mother, suggests that the period was neither easy nor particularly satisfying for her.

Mrs Thatcher's fortunes improved at the age of 41 when she began a five-year single positive period ruled by Mercury (1966-71). She served with distinction in Edward Heath's government (1970-74), which overlapped the start of her six-year double positive Venus period in 1971. After the Conservatives' 1974 electoral defeat she stood as party leader, which she became in 1975, at 49. The double positive period ended on her 52nd birthday in 1977, but was immediately followed by another, a four-year period ruled by the Negative Sun (1977-81) and linked with her 4 birth number. It was during this period, in 1979 at age 53, that Mrs Thatcher became Prime Minister.

Mrs Thatcher began a Mars-ruled single negative period on her 56th birthday in 1981 and this will run for nine years until her 65th birthday in 1990. In all probability this period won't be as successful for her as the two previous periods, despite the increased popularity she gained as a result of the 1982 Falklands Crisis and her resounding election victory of 1983. Indeed, she will need to guide the Ship of State with great care if she is to save both it and herself from the rocks.

5

NUMBERS AND PATHWAYS

Just as your birth number creates the good, the bad and the neutral periods of our life, so it also gives your life direction. Birth presents the individual with a bewildering range of possibilities which are narrowed down by the birth number, to give you or anyone else a reduced number of pathways to follow. Thus the individual is free, but not entirely free. He or she can make choices but the choices are restricted.

Such pathways are by no means limited to only one birth number. In fact, they often join with those originating from other numbers, forming common routes down which many can pass. But the going is not equally easy for all. Some will find the way straight and smooth, while others will have difficult time of it. And some won't get started at all. To them the way is effectively barred.

An example will make this clear. Since the Second World War, Great Britain has had nine different prime ministers: Clement Attlee, Winston Churchill, Anthony Eden, Harold MacMillan, Alec Douglas-Home, Harold Wilson, Edward Heath, James Callaghan and Margaret Thatcher. We might expect, if the birth number is entirely unrelated to one's path in life, these nine to have a varied selection of birth numbers, not all nine perhaps, but two of one, two of another, one of this and one of that, etc. But nothing could be further from the truth. The nine prime ministers each have either a 4 birth number, a 6 birth number or a 7 birth number.

The actual birth numbers possessed by each are: Clement Attlee, 6; Winston Churchill, 7; Anthony Eden, 7; Harold MacMillan, 7; Alec Douglas-Home, 4; Harold Wilson, 4, Edward Heath, 6; James Callaghan, 7; and Margaret Thatcher, 4.

Four prime ministers had a 7 birth number, three had (or have) a 4 birth number and two had a 6 birth number. Thus, judged on this group of post-war prime ministers, it would seem that the pathway to premiership is only open to those with a 4, 6 or 7 birth number, and that the going is easiest for those with a 7 birth number, somewhat harder for those with a 4 birth number, and hardest for those with a 6 birth number.

If we examine the birth numbers of the remaining twentieth-century British prime ministers we find that while other numbers do turn up, there is still a bias in favour of 4, 6 and 7. These are the birth numbers of the other prime ministers of this century: Archibald Rosebury, 5; Arthur Balfour, 8; Henry Campbell-Bannerman, 7; Herbert Asquith, 1; David Lloyd George, 9; Andrew Bonar Law, 2; Stanley Baldwin, 6; Ramsay MacDonald, 7; and Neville Chamberlain, 9.

Out of this total of eighteen people who reached the highest political office in the land, six had a 7 birth number, three a 4 birth number, three a 6 birth number, two a 9 birth number, one a 1 birth number, one a 2 birth number, one a 5 birth number and one an 8 birth number. No prime minister had a 3 birth number. This demonstrates that while the pathway to Number 10 is very difficult to negotiate for those with a 1, 2, 5 or an 8 birth number, it is impassible for those having a birth number of 3.

Despite the good intentions of those entering politics, it remains a dirty business. Those that get to the top are the toughest, sharpest and most ambitious of the lot. Luck plays its part, yet it is a particular personality that wins the olive wreath. It therefore isn't surprising that those with a 7 birth number are most likely to succeed. 7 is the number of the Negative Moon and it gives its possessor access to those negative qualities stemming from the dark side of the Moon, such as duplicity, stealth, guile and charm, as well as the power of hypnotic influence. And because 7 is the number of death, it is, like death, 'all-conquering' – or, at least, very nearly. Likewise, 4 is the number of the Negative Sun, the number of the Sun descending towards the underworld, and its qualities of strength and determination are admixed with the darker ones of ruthless ambition and the need to be in charge. No one can deny the attractiveness and charm of Alec Douglas-Home, Harold Wilson and Margaret Thatcher, each of whom has a 4 birth number, or the mailed fist that each conceals in a velvet glove. The other number bringing greatest success in British politics is 6, the number of Venus, which is, like 7, a number of the underworld. For while we now think of Venus as the most delightful of the ancient goddesses, she in fact had two sides: she was a love goddess and a war goddess, just as her planet appears as the lucky morning star and as the malevolent evening star. Thus despite the beauty and artistic talents of those born with a 6 birth number, such people are the possessors of altogether darker gifts.

In the United States, where good looks and a pleasing personality are more important in political life than they are in Britain, those with a 6 birth number have the most success in getting into the White House. Indeed, of the sixteen presidents that America has had this century, four have had a 6 birth number, the last being Richard Nixon. In second place come those with a 2 birth number, of whom there have been three, the most recent being Ronald Reagan. However, the possession of a 7 birth number, which is so important for political success in Britain, gives no more advantage than a birth number of 5, 8 or 9, each of which have belonged to two presidents. Yet it is significant that the two presidents who had a 7 birth number – Harry S. Truman and John F. Kennedy – were the most memorable.

In strange contrast to the British experience, a 4 birth number works against those hoping to become President, for nobody having this number has reached the White House this century. The American people don't care for the concealed, yet evident ruthlessness of the Negative Moon.

But as in Britain, those born with a 3 birth number don't make it to the top of the political tree either. This century has produced no presidents with such a birth number. Thus it's thumbs down on both sides of the Atlantic for the poor 3s. Indeed, Edward Kennedy (birth number 3) was perhaps wiser than we think when he withdrew from the last presidential election.

It is now time to describe the chief pathways belonging to each of the nine birth numbers. But first it must be pointed out that because the birth number represents certain character traits possessed by its owner, these will either be the same as or similar to the ego character delineated by the vowel number or quite different. If your birth number is the same as your vowel number, then the description of your character traits and job preferences given below will be exact. But if they are different you should take the information given for your birth number as your primary guide and that given for your vowel as your secondary guide. The truth will be a mix of the two.

If your birth number is 1: 1 is the number of the Positive Sun and gives you the twin advantages of self-confidence and self-assurance. You are determined and resourceful, and you are quick to make the most of whatever opportunities come your way. These traits, combined with your solar energy, aggression and desire to succeed, help you get to the top, which is where you believe you deserve to be. You enjoy being in charge: you like organizing, directing and giving orders. And because you believe in yourself and your ideas, you are not shy of taking responsibility and making decisions. Yet you are by no means power-mad, and your innate sympathy and understanding usually enable you to enjoy good relations with your subordinates. Also, you are fortunate in being able to instil confidence and provide inspiration. Because you work hard and have clear goals, you always stand a good chance of getting where you want to be. Your chief fault is your extravagance, thus you should avoid handling other people's money. Other handicaps include your conservatism and your gullibility. You are attracted to and function well in all areas of business and commerce, the Church, the legal profession, local politics, political science, community work, teaching and lecturing, government service, medicine (especially the care of the heart and blood system), public relations and any occupation having to do with gold. You also enjoy involvement in trade unions, working for royalty or the aristocracy in a supervisory capacity, and participation in those artistic activities such as acting, which can bring both fame and financial reward. In a similar way you are attracted to military service. In short, you want to be respected, honoured and appreciated.

If your birth number is 2: 2 is the number of the Positive Moon and gives you both a rising spirit and the important quality of quiet persistence. You are not, however, as go-getting as those with a 1 birth number, thus you seldom desire the top job. You get on well with other people and you usually enjoy good relations with your workmates. Indeed, you prefer working with others than by yourself. Your natural concern for your fellows inclines you to work for charities, clinics or hospitals, or as a social worker, counsellor or probation officer – that is, in some role that allows you to be of service to others. In a similar way, your unique ability to understand the point of view and the problems of others, makes you a natural diplomat, advisor and mediator. Because you also have a good imagination and artistic talent, you are drawn to work in advertising, interior and architectural design, public relations, painting and decorating, and also to the legal profession, journalism, the Church, catering, domestic work, building, estate agencing, buying and selling antiques and second-hand goods, farming, bartending, waiting, teaching and anything to do with the sea and with fluids. Ideally, you want to give rather than to receive and to be valued for yourself.

If your birth number is 3: 3 is the number of Jupiter and it marks you out as a higher soul, as someone who is less concerned with selfish ends than with promoting justice, helping others and increasing knowledge. Your kindly and generous character stops you from doing work that is at all dishonest or disreputable, or that requires you to be pushy and assertive. Yet your love of travel and change makes you avoid those jobs that are dull and repetitive, or which tie you down. You are naturally optimistic and cheerful, and you rarely flinch from taking on something that others find too difficult. Because you enjoy being outdoors, you are attracted to any work that gets you outside, particularly if this involves sport, animals or defending your country. You are also interested in community work, the Church, teaching and academic research, medicine and hospital work, editing and publishing, writing, civil engineering, the civil service, insurance, archaeology, music, dowsing and mediumship, geology, travel agencing, hairstyling, the sale of drugs and chemicals, copy-writing, hotel work and herbalism. But no matter what job you do you will always strive to increase your knowledge through study, just as you will always adhere to your religious beliefs.

If your birth number is 4: 4 is the number of the Negative Sun and it gives you a friendly public face which masks a deeper, more complex hidden person. This means that despite your friendliness you are very detached, and indeed you place great importance on your independence. You hate being tied down or ordered about, thus you are only really happy in a job which allows you to be your own boss. You benefit from your solar energy, which enables you to keep plugging away at something long after others would have called it a day. This can, however, be both a strength and a weakness, for sometimes you refuse to give up despite there being no chance of success. Indeed, you are motivated chiefly by the desire for success, which goads you constantly like a spur. You are attracted to those occupations that allow you to be both independent and creative, thus freelance creative work is ideal for you, such as freelance photography, journalism, song-writing, designing, entertaining, etc. You are also drawn to the occult and to anything strange or bizarre, as well as to astronomy and science, dancing and choreography, theatre direction and singing, writing and publishing, engineering, computing, anything electrical, banking, surveying, psychiatry, the post office and railways, teaching, laboratory work, politics and office work. Because self-realization is so important to you, you care very little about what others think of you. You always try to do your own thing.

If your birth number is 5: 5 is the number of Mercury and it indicates you have a quick, active brain, a persuasive tongue and a desire to get ahead. You function best in jobs that allow you to use your wits and your powers of persuasion, thus manual work or work that is uninteresting is not for you. You also require plenty of change and variety in your work and this can lead you to change your job quite often. You will also moonlight if the opportunity arises. But you are not overly ambitious and you do not want to be encumbered with heavy responsibilities. Your anxious disposition may make you too fussy and too preoccupied with details, which can have a deleterious effect on your working relationships. Yet you generally get on well with others, for you prefer to work as part of a team rather than alone. The following jobs are examples of those that both attract you and which can give you fulfilment: salesman, journalist, writer, teacher or instructor, tour guide, advertising copy-writer, public relations consultant, lawyer, government official, political scientist, engineer, radio and television announcer, record producer, actor, courier, taxi-driver, transport manager, architect and inventor. You will inevitably face set-backs and disappointments in your career, but your high spirits and ready sense of fun will help you to cope with these.

If your birth number is 6: 6 is the number of Venus and it indicates that you have a natural distaste for any job that is dirty and unpleasant. Thus, in general, manual work does not appeal to you. Your friendly and easy manner enables you to get on well with others, to the extent that you seldom have conflicts with your colleagues. Although you like the outdoors and anything to do with farming and gardening, you are drawn to jobs that are glamorous, such as those connected with the arts, with fashion and beauty, and with health care. You have a talent for buying and selling, for arbitration and for pleasing others. You also enjoy acting as an intermediary, which is required in public relations, law and diplomacy. You don't, however, like work that is too taxing, for you are rather lazy. But you do like money and you expect to be well-paid for what you do. Generally speaking, you favour those jobs that bring you into contact with the public and which allow you to exercise certain skills, such as hairdressing, massage, social work, sports training, decorating and designing, selling perfume and cosmetics, art work and stationery, publishing, engraving, pawnbroking, bartending and retailing second-hand goods. But you should be aware of your darker side which could, in the wrong circumstances, lead you into pornography, drug-dealing and prostitution.

If your birth number is 7: 7 is the number of the Negative Moon and it reveals that you have a rather romantic attitude to life as well as strange yearnings. You have a restless disposition, which not only prompts you to change your job quite often but makes you impatient with anything that stops you going forwards as fast as you would like. Because your colleagues tend to misunderstand you, your relations with them are often fraught. You like having money, yet you are careless with it, hence you should avoid handling other people's money. You are imaginative and creative, but although you can work hard to achieve a particular goal, you dislike discipline and routine. You are attracted to glamorous jobs, such as those connected with the arts or with entertainment, and to politics, community work and academic research, to maritime activities (especially those having to do with overseas trade), and to any work that is theoretical rather than practical. Your interest in the welfare of others can lead you into medicine (you are fascinated by disorders of the nervous system), nursing, social work, veterinary science, chiropody, chiropractym and the rehabilitation of those with drink or drug problems. Also, you enjoy writing, trade union activities, selling drugs and medicines, playing a musical instrument, and restaurant work. Your sensitivity to the needs of others and your natural psychic gifts give you an almost mystical power, which can, of course, be used for either good or evil.

If your birth number is 8: 8 is the number of Saturn and it indicates that you have a sober and practical approach to life. Your logical and analytical brain enables you to plan and organize; it also allows you to take responsibility. You are patient, persistent and ambitious, thus you are quite capable of working towards long-term goals. Indeed, you rarely expect overnight success.

Additionally, you have a good memory, a talent for languages and an ability to keep your temper. Despite the fact that you are a loner, you get on well with others, especially if they are older than you. The sort of job that most attracts you is one that both offers security and the chance to move ahead. But you are paradoxical in that although you are conservative and conventional, your type of job can be drawn from a very wide field. You are interested in commerce and government service, building and architectural design, mining and farming, science and engineering, law and police work, musical composition and singing (you are blessed with an excellent voice), dentistry and medicine (especially disorders of the bones and skin), boxing, both as a fighter and promoter, estate agencing, funeral directing, computer programming and systems analysis. You are the archetypal strong, silent type and you set your goals when you are quite young: you then dedicate your life to achieving them.

If your birth number is 9: 9 is the number of Mars and it reveals that you have a complex character, because it marks the end of one solar cycle and the start of another. Thus while you are mature and wise, you also have a youthful naïvety and a restless desire for adventure. In a similar way you are selfish and aggressive, but also introspective and uncertain. Yet your readiness to get up and get going makes you a pioneer, and your enthusiasm for the task ahead gives inspiration to others. Less happily, you lose interest quickly and so seldom complete what you begin. Because you are very independent and like being in charge, you hate any work that puts you in a subservient role. You are attracted to the Armed Forces, although you would not wish to remain a foot soldier, and to the manufacture of weapons and machine tools. You are likewise interested in surgery and medical research (especially that relating to cancer, blood ailments and bowel and bladder disorders), science (especially biology, genetics and physics), advertising, banking, stockbroking, insurance, accountancy, acting and entertaining, butchering, sport and farming, and to hunting, animal-training and zoo-keeping. You love tinkering with machinery and you enjoy fixing things. But despite all your energy and enthusiasm you are always aware that you could be doing better.

6

NUMBER-RHYTHMS

In Chapter Four it was shown how everyone's life is made up of an alternating series of positive, negative and neutral periods, which can be determined by using the birth number and the solar cycle. The shortest of these periods lasts for one year (a 1 or Positive Sun period) and the longest for nine years (a 9 or Mars period). Quite often periods having a similar value follow one another, to give an extended positive, negative or neutral period. For example, those with a birth number of 1 or 9 enjoy three consecutive double positive periods between the ages of 13 and 26, while those with a 5 birth number experience three double negative periods running consecutively at this time, which is why their teens and years of early adulthood are so difficult.

But the terms 'positive', 'negative' and 'neutral' only apply to the period they describe as a whole, not to all of the days that make it up. Thus while a double positive period may bring the happiest moments, the best opportunities and the greatest triumphs of a person's life, some of its individual days will be difficult and some unhappy. And likewise, a double negative period has plenty of days that contrast with its overall nature and which in fact make it bearable.

Indeed, each life period is made up of good or positive days, bad or negative days and neutral days. Of course, the best days are the good days of a double positive period, the worst are the bad days of a double negative period. The wise man and woman will take maximum advantage of the former and be extra careful on the latter.

The first step in determining the nature of any day is to reduce its date to a single number. Let us take as our example 10 June 1984. Because June is the sixth month of the year this date reduces as follows:

$$1 + 0 + 6 + 1 + 9 + 8 + 4 = 29$$
$$2 + 9 = 11$$
$$1 + 1 = 2$$

10 June 1984 is thus a 2 day. How it will respond to you depends on your birth number, for days are like the life periods: they can either be single positive or double positive, single negative or double negative, or neutral. In fact any day will be all of these to people with different birth numbers. This explains why a day that is good for me may be bad for you.

To discover the nature of any day we must again refer to the solar cycle, except that this time we have to turn the 'number wheel' to bring your birth number to the westerly sunset position, whose value is double negative. Thus it is the sunrise position which determines the life periods and the sunset position the day type. Let us suppose that you have a 3 birth number. This is how the solar cycle arranges itself for you:

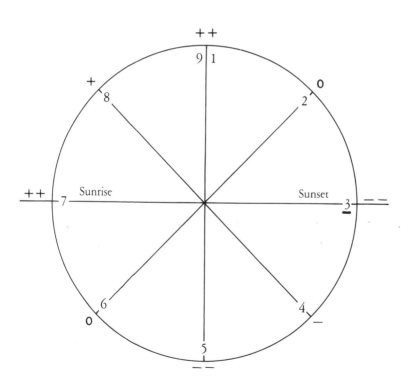

Because 2 is placed against a neutral point this indicates that any date that reduces to 2 – and hence 10 June 1984 – is a neutral day for you. Likewise, those dates that reduce to 1 and 9 are double positive, those that reduce to 3 are double negative, those that reduce to 4 are single negative, those that reduce to 5 are double negative, those that reduce to 6 are neutral, those that reduce to 7 are double positive, and those that reduce to 8 are single positive.

By turning the other numbers to the western horizon, we can in a similar manner determine the nature of any day or date for each birth number. These day values are summarized in the table below:

Birth Number

	1	2	3	4	5	6	7	8	9
1	--	0	++	+	++	0	--	-	--
2	-	--	0	++	+	++	0	--	-
3	--	-	--	0	++	+	++	0	--
4	0	--	-	--	0	++	+	++	0
5	++	0	--	-	--	0	++	+	++
6	+	++	0	--	-	--	0	++	+
7	++	+	++	0	--	-	--	0	++
8	0	++	+	++	0	--	-	--	0
9	--	0	++	+	++	0	--	-	--

Date Number (label at left of rows 4–5)

Because every date can be reduced to one of the nine single numbers, this means that behind every date sequence lies a cycle of enneads, which in turn gives a recurring cycle of positive, negative and neutral days which is unique to each birth number, with the exception of 1 and 9, which share the same place in the solar cycle and thus the same days.

These cycles form a background rhythm to human life which are, with their constant risings and fallings, very similar to bio-rhythms. For this reason, we can call them *number-rhythms*. At the top of the next page for example, is the number-rhythm cycle of someone who has a 3 birth number.

And beneath is the number-rhythm cycle of someone with a 1 or 9 birth number.

Generally speaking, we feel at our best mentally and physically

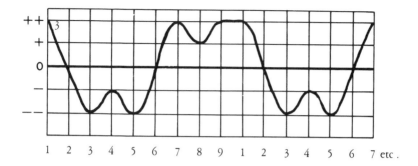

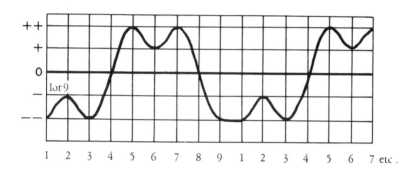

on positive days and at our worst on negative days. Positive days are also potentially luckier. They are the days when things tend to go right for us, when we make a better impression on others and when, sometimes, our dreams come true. By contrast, negative days are potentially less fortunate. They are the days when we tend to make mistakes, when we have difficulties with others and when our schemes fail. And on double negative days we are more likely to have accidents, sometimes fatal ones. For example, Buddy Holly (birth number 8), the singer, died in a plane crash on what was for him a double negative day, 3 February 1959. A double negative day was also unfortunate for President Richard Nixon (birth number 6). It was on such a day – 17 June 1972 – that the Watergate conspirators were arrested, an event which led directly to his impeachment. Similarly, Elvis Presley (birth number 9) died suddenly on one of his double negative days, 16 August 1977.

One is also more likely to die violently on a double negative day. President James Garfield (birth number 7) was assassinated on such a day – 19 September 1881 – as was President John Kennedy (birth number 7), who was shot by Lee Harvey Oswald on 22 November 1963.

But although the risk of accidental or violent death is higher on a double negative day, this is not to say that death always occurs on negative days, whether these be single negative or double negative. Death is not, *per se*, a negative experience. It is as much a part of life as birth, thus when it happens naturally at the end of a long life it must surely be regarded as a positive event. This is why America's oldest man John B. Salling (birth number 1), who died at 113, left this world on one of his double positive days, 16 March 1959.

Thus, no matter what your birth number, each day that you live through will be potentially either good (+) or very good (++), bad (−) or very bad (−−), or neutral (0). The key word here is 'potentially'. Days are like wound springs, most of which never unwind. Yet if the right action is performed on the right day, the result can be marvellous, while if the wrong action is performed on the wrong day, a catastrophe can occur. This is why one should only take risks on positive days, never on negative days. Neutral days are usually just that, uneventful and unexciting. But surprises do sometimes happen on them, not all of them nice. Film-star James Dean (birth number 6) crashed his Porsche and killed himself on one of his neutral days, 30 September 1955, while President William McKinley (birth number 1) was shot by the anarchist Leon Czolgosz on one of his, 6 September 1901.

However, the number-rhythm cycles do not flow smoothly throughout the entire year because they are interrupted at the end of every month. For example, take 31 December 1984, which reduces to 2:

$$3+1+1+2+1+9+8+4=29$$
$$2+9=11$$
$$1+1=\ 2$$

But the following day, 1 January 1985, reduces to 7:

$$1+1+1+9+8+5=25$$
$$2+5=\ 7$$

This means that from Christmas Day, 25 December 1984 (which reduces to 5) to 6 January 1985 (which reduces to 3) the number sequence runs:

5 6 7 8 9 1 2 / 7 8 9 1 2 3, etc.

This particular interruption will be to the advantage of some number types, who will gain a longer positive period because of it, but to the disadvantage of others, who will be subjected to an extra-long negative period. Thus the period between Christmas Day 1984 and Twelfth Night 1985 was fortunate for those with a 3 birth number but unfortunate for those with a 7 birth number, as the graph below illustrates:

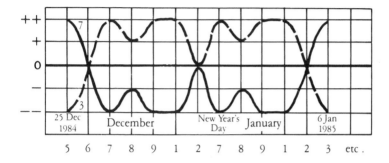

This graph also shows that the number-rhythms of those with a 3 birth number and those with a 7 birth number are mirror images of each other. Thus when the 3's have positive days the 7's have negative days, and vice versa. This 'mirror image' effect happens to those numbers that stand opposite each other in the solar cycle. It is most clearly seen in the graph below, which shows the uninterrupted number rhythms of those having a 4 birth number and those having an 8 birth number:

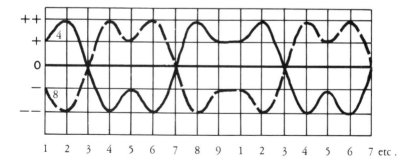

In fact, such number-rhythms are complementary. For although the 4s are at their worst on days four, five and 6, their low spirits are matched by the more buoyant mood of the 8s on these days. The reverse is true on days one, two, eight and nine, when the 4s are at their best and the 8s at their worst. In the first instance the 8s will be able to shrug their shoulders at the cranky 4s, whereas the reverse will be true in the second. On two days, however, their moods exactly coincide, for on days three and seven they are both in neutral. They will then be able to settle any differences that may have arisen between them.

But now compare the number-rhythms of those with a 5 birth number and those with a 6 birth number:

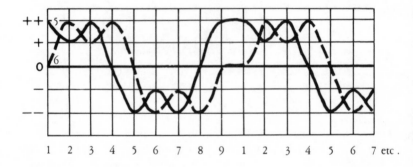

In this case the number-rythms closely coincide, so that both have up-swings and down-swings together. On no day are their moods ever identical. Thus 5 and 6 types get on well on days two and three, when both have their moods uplifted by what is for them either a single positive day or a double positive day. The same is true, although to a lesser degree, on days one and four, when one of them enjoys a double positive day and the other has a neutral day. Their number-rhythms work against them, however, on days five, six, seven and eight, when the mood of one or the other is always depressed by a double negative day, while that of the other is never lifted above neutral. This produces a tense period when arguments and disagreements are likely to occur. Hence we can summarize the character of the relationship between those with a 5 birth number and those with a 6 birth number as unstable. For while 4s and 8s are true opposites, whose balanced opposition can lead to mutual respectd and friendship, the 5s and the 6s are never in 'synch'. Indeed, their low periods can engender sufficient hostility to neutralize the effect of their positive periods. They tend therefore to become polarized and to avoid one another. They have no common ground in an emotional sense on which they can build friendship.

But what of those with a 1 or a 9 birth number, who have identical number-rhythms, or those who have the same birth number? How do they get on together?

The answer, quite simply, is well. For because their moods exactly coincide, they experience the same peaks and slumps. Thus they feel kindred spirits, which is of course, what they are. They will get on famously on those days which are single positive or double positive for them, while on single negative days or double negative days they will either keep themselves to themselves to avoid conflict or they will commiserate with each other because they know how the other feels.

From this we can conclude that we get on best with those who have the same birth number as ourselves or whose birth number lies opposite ours in the solar cycle, 1 and 9 being the opposites of 5, 2 the opposite of 6, 3 of 7, and 4 of 8. Likewise, we also enjoy quite good relations with those whose birth number stands at right angles to our own in the solar cycle. Consider, for example, the number-rhythms of those possessing a 2 birth number and those possessing an 8 birth number, which are shown below:

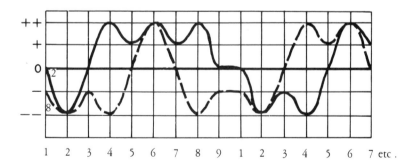

Here we see an exact correlation of mood on day two, which is double negative for both, and on day six, which is double positive for them, while on days four and eight their moods are polarized. As we saw earlier, such mood matchings promote good relations, thus we can expect the two types either to get on well or to sensibly shun each each other on these days. They will also enjoy tolerably good relations on days five and seven, when the mood of one is single positive and that of the other is neutral. The only danger days are one, three and nine, when the irritated single negative mood of the one could provoke anger in the neutral, and therefore unstable, mood of the other.

But the situation is complicated by the fact that the number rhythms work against a background provided by the life periods, whose own nature can either be positive, negative or neutral. This means that if we take the days of a neutral period as representing the norm, then those of a positive period are potentially better and those of a negative period are potentially worse. Hence the days with the greatest potential are the double positive days of a double positive life period, whilst those with the worst potential are the double negative days of a double negative period.

Yet quite often the nature of a day can override that of the period in which it falls, which is why good things can happen in negative periods and bad things in positive periods. For example, Russian cosmonaut Yuri Gargarin (birth number 2) was launched into space on one of his double positive days, 12 April 1961, and became the first man to orbit the earth despite the double negative life period he was then undergoing. And French aviator Louis Bleriot (birth number 8) successfully flew the English Channel on what was for him a double positive day, 25 July 1909, even though he made the attempt in a neutral period.

Similarly, the nature of the period can outweigh that of its days. President Abraham Lincoln (birth number 5) was assassinated during a double negative period, yet on a day that was for him single positive, 14 April 1865. Martin Luther King (birth number 1) was even more unfortunate. He was shot to death during a double negative period, yet on a day that was for him double positive, 4 April 1968. Contrariwise, Roger Bannister (birth number 2) became the first man to run a mile in under four minutes on 6 May 1954. This was a single negative day for him but fortunately the attempt was made during a single positive period. And Charles Lindbergh (birth number 9) took off to fly the Atlantic on one of his neutral days – 20 May 1927 – and successfully landed in France on the following day, which was for him a double negative one. However, he was lucky enough to have made the attempt in a double positive life period.

Because the life periods can last a maximum of nine years and because their nature is representative of the period as a whole rather than parts of it, individual days often express themselves more forcibly than might be expected. This accounts for the success that some people enjoy when in competition with others who are undergoing a more positive life period. Such people win because the day is right for them.

In this respect it is salutary to examine the fortunes of political rivals. In British general elections, for example, the chief combatants are the Prime Minister and the Leader of the Opposition, who compete against each other both as individuals and as symbols of all that their own political parties have to offer the electorate.

In 1945 the two contestants were Winston Churchill (birth number 7) and Clement Attlee (birth number 6). Both had, as we have already discovered, strong birth numbers for political success, yet Churchill was favoured by his formidable war record and by the single positive period (1942-50) he was then undergoing. Attlee, by contrast, was in a nine-year neutral period (1939-48). But despite Churchill's advantages he suffered a stunning election defeat. Yet this was not so surprising when we consider the date on which the election was held, 26 July 1945. This was a double negative day for Churchill, but only a neutral one for Attlee.

The two contended again in 1950. Churchill was then nearing the end of his single positive period (1942-50) and Attlee was undergoing a three-year single negative period he had started in 1948. The election took place on 23 February 1950, which was a double positive day for Attlee and a single positive day for Churchill. Attlee won.

The two leaders fought each other for the third and last time on 25 October 1951. Churchill was then living through a neutral period (1950-52), while Attlee had begun an advantageous double positive period (1951-9). But the date was in Churchill's favour, being neutral for him and double negative for Attlee. Churchill won the election and remained Prime Minister until his retirement in 1955.

In the general election of 1955 Clement Attlee fought against the new Tory leader, Anthony Eden (birth number 7). Both men were evenly matched as far as their life periods were concerned as each was running a double positive period (Eden 1953-62; Attlee 1951-9). But again it was the nature of the day that determined the election outcome. The election date – 26 May 1955 – was neutral for Eden and double negative for Attlee. Not surprisingly, Eden won.

The general election of 1959 brought two new men into

conflict – Conservative Prime Minister Harold MacMillan (birth number 7), who had taken office when Anthony Eden resigned, and Labour leader Hugh Gaitskell (birth number 2). This was an election, judged on day and period strength, that Gaitskell should have won. The date – 8 October 1959 – was double positive for Gaitskell and neutral for MacMillan. Gaitskell was then running a double positive period (1958-62), while MacMillan had just started a double negative period (1959-62). Yet the victor was Harold MacMillan, who romped home by a mile. But how did he do it? The answer lies in his 7 birth number, which is incomparably stronger for gaining political success than Gaitskell's weak 2. Indeed, only one prime minister of this century has had a 2 birth number and he – Andrew Bonar Law – stayed in office for just seven months.

The general election of 1964 pitted Tory prime minister Alec Douglas-Home (birth number 4) against the Labour leader Harold Wilson (birth number 4). Because both men had the same birth number this meant that the election date – 15 October 1964 – was single positive for both of them. Thus the prize had to go to the man with the life period advantage. Harold Wilson was then enjoying a double positive period (1962-8), while Alec Douglas-Home was in the middle of a single negative period (1959-68). The Labour Party and Harold Wilson won the election. But it was close. The new government only had a majority of five.

The contenders in the election of 1970 were Harold Wilson and the new Tory leader Edward Heath (birth number 6). Wilson was then running a double positive life period (1968-72), which gave him an advantage over Heath, who was undergoing a double negative period (1968-72). But the election date – 17 June 1970 – was strongly in Heath's favour, being double positive for him but double negative for Wilson. The winner was Edward Heath.

The date decided the contest four years later when the same pair again competed for office. This time Heath was in a neutral life period (1972-81), which gave him a slight advantage over Wilson, who was running a single negative period (1972-81). But the election date – 2 March 1974 – was double negative for Heath and double positive for Wilson. Wilson won.

The general election of 1979 was made doubly interesting by the fact that for the first time in British history the Conservative leader was a woman – Margaret Thatcher (birth number 4). Her opponent was the Labour prime minister James Callaghan (birth number 7). But despite Callaghan having the stronger birth number, everything else was in Mrs Thatcher's favour. For not only was she undergoing a double positive life period (1977-81), in contrast to the double negative one that Callaghan was running (1977-80), but the date chosen for the election – 4 May 1979 – was also double positive for her, yet single negative for him. Hardly surprisingly, Mrs Thatcher won hands down.

The most recent general election took place on 9 June 1983. It pitted Mrs Thatcher against the new Labour leader Michael Foot (birth number 8). Foot had the advantage in that he was two years into a double positive life period (1981-9), while Mrs Thatcher had begun a long single negative period (1981-90). The date, however, was favourable to Mrs Thatcher, being single positive for her but single negative for Michael Foot. Yet it wasn't really this that won the election for her. Her victory really stemmed from Foot's weak birth number, which meant that had the election taken place on a double positive day for him he would still have lost. He was, judged on his birth number, a non-starter.

These post-war election contests show that victory at the ballot box in Britain goes to the party leader who has a strong birth number (4, 6 or 7), who is living through a positive life period and who is lucky enough to have the election called on a date that is positive, preferably double positive, for him.

But what of the future, especially now that the traditional two-party system has been upset by the emergence of the SDP/Liberal Alliance? Well, none of this makes any difference because the person who is to become the next prime minister will be decided by the factors mentioned above. Let us therefore examine the likely challengers to Mrs Thatcher in the election of 1987 or 1988.

The new leader of the Labour Party is Neil Kinnock, who was born on 28 March 1942. This gives him a 2 birth number:

$$2+8+3+1+9+4+2=29$$
$$2+9=11$$
$$1+1=2$$

Kinnock is now running a neutral life period which will last until his birthday in 1988 (1983-8). It will then be followed by a double negative period (1988-94).

The leader of the SDP is Dr David Owen, who was born on 2 July 1938, a date that gives him a 3 birth number:

$$2+7+1+9+3+8=30$$
$$3+0=3$$

On his 46th birthday in 1984 Dr Owen started a neutral life period which will run until his 52nd birthday in 1990.

Lastly, David Steele is the current leader of the Liberal Party. He was born on 31 March 1938 and thus has a 1 birth number:

$$3 + 1 + 3 + 1 + 9 + 3 + 8 = 28$$
$$2 + 8 = 10$$
$$1 + 0 = 1$$

Steele began a single negative life period on his birthday in 1984. This will run until his birthday in 1990.

Because Mrs Thatcher is also undergoing a single negative life period which will last until 1990, this means that none of the probable contenders in the 1987/88 general election will have a strong life period advantage. However, should the election be held in the summer of 1988 Dr Owen, who will be in a neutral life period, will be slightly ahead of the rest of the field.

The destiny of these people thus lies in their birth numbers, so what hope can they find in them? Well, for the three men not much. David Owen, who has a 3 birth number, can be immediately given the thumbs down. His birth number, as we have already seen, is a complete non-starter. And Kinnock's 2 is little better. It is a decidedly weak number to field against the strong 4 belonging to Mrs Thatcher and it almost certainly spells defeat for the Labour Party.

That leaves David Steele. His 1 birth number is not a weak one like Owen's and Kinnock's, for although only one prime minister this century has had such a birth number – Herbert Asquith – he held office for an astonishing eight years (1908-16). But even so it cannot match the strength of Mrs Thatcher's 4 birth number. And that means that if Margaret Hilda Thatcher is still the Conservative leader at the next election there can be no doubt that she will win.

At least, just as long as she chooses a date that is double positive for her!

7

YOUR NUMBER ACCORD

In our discussion of numbers and destiny we have seen how your birth number determines your life periods and your number rhythms. But while this is useful and practical knowledge, it cannot tell you if your life will be happy and successful. For everyone with the same birth number has the same sequence of life periods and the same number rhythms, yet the quality of their lives can vary greatly.

So can numerology lift the last of Fortuna's veils and show you the future? Can it tell you if your life will be happy or sad, fulfilling or unfulfilling, successful or unsuccessful?

Yes, it can. And it can do more than that. It can also help you to change the direction of your life so that it follows a happier and more satisfying course.

In this respect numerology is unique. No other method of prediction allows the individual to alter his destiny, for they are mere passive announcers of what will be. And this applies as much to astrology as it does to the reading of tea leaves.

This flexibility arises from the two sorts of numbers that are important to us. On the one hand we have our birth number, which is fixed by fate and cannot be changed, while on the other we have our name numbers, which can be changed simply by changing our names.

Of the three name numbers – the vowel number, the consonant number and the name number itself – it is the last which is most important to us in terms of life success. For it is the accord that exists between it and the unchangeable birth number which determines how happy and fulfilled our lives will be.

To understand how this accord is established it is necessary to examine the diagram at the top of page 98 which shows the positive, negative and neutral areas of the solar cycle.

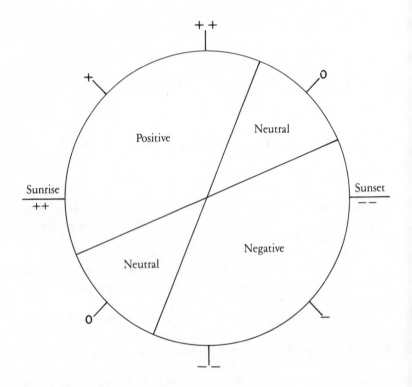

Let us now suppose that you have a 6 birth number and an 8 name number. To find out the accord that they enjoy, the 'number wheel' must be turned to bring your birth number to the sunrise position. We then note the placement of the 8 (see page 99).

Because the 8 falls in the positive area, this means that there is a *positive accord* between your birth number and your name number. The same accord would exist if your name number was 6 or 7 because these also lie in the positive area. Such an accord indicates that your life will be happy and satisfying.

If you had the same birth number – 6 – but a name number that was 1, 5 or 9, then because these all lie in the two neutral areas there would exist a *neutral accord* between your birth number and your name number. This would mean that your life will be moderately happy and satisfying.

However, had you the same birth number but a name number that was 2, 3 or 4, which lie in the negative area, then a *negative accord* would exist between your birth number and your name

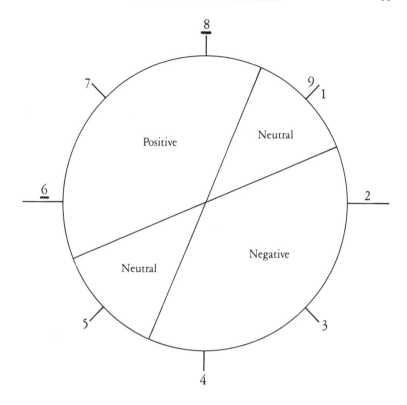

number. This would show that your life will not be happy and satisfying.

The accord that exists between the birth number and the name number indicates how successful one's life will be in terms of happiness and personal satisfaction, not its success in a material sense. Sometimes, of course, all these go together, so that one becomes rich, famous and happy. But this is an extremely rare state. Riches and fame tend to drive away happiness, not attract it.

For example, let us again consider Elvis Presley, the late King of Rock 'n' Roll, who had a 9 birth number. His name number was 5:

ELVIS PRESLEY
5 3 4 9 1 7 9 5 1 3 5 7 = 59 = 14 = 5

But although Elvis Presley was the most famous popular singer of this century, the accord that existed between his birth number and his name number was *negative* (see page 101).

This reveals that despite his great fame and wealth, Elvis

Presley was not a happy or a fulfilled man. And, indeed, a recent biography has described him as psychologically troubled, sexually deviant and physically ill, as well as being a drug addict. He also died prematurely at the age of 42.

If you have calculated your birth number and your name number, the table below will enable you to determine quickly the accord that exists between them, and thus, as a result, the quality of your life.

Name Numbers

		Positive	Neutral	Negative
	1	1, 2, 3, 9	4, 8	5, 6, 7
	2	2, 3, 4	1, 5, 9	6, 7, 8
	3	3, 4, 5	2, 6	1, 7, 8, 9
Birth	4	4, 5, 6	3, 7	1, 2, 8, 9
Numbers	5	5, 6, 7	4, 8	1, 2, 3, 9
	6	6, 7, 8	1, 5, 9	2, 3, 4
	7	1, 7, 8, 9	2, 6	3, 4, 5
	8	1, 2, 8, 9	3, 7	4, 5, 6
	9	1, 2, 3, 9	4, 8	5, 6, 7

Let us now examine the accord that exists between the birth number and the name number of some well-known people, to see whether or not it reflects the apparent quality of their lives.

As our first example, we will take the nine men and women who have become prime ministers of post-war Britain. All were successful in their political life and, at least as far as is known, in their family and social life. We would therefore expect, on this basis, for them to have a positive accord between their birth number and their name number.

The first post-war prime minister was Clement Attlee, who was born on 3 January 1883. This gave him a 6 birth number. His name number is 9:

CLEMENT ATTLEE
3 3 5 4 5 5 2 1 2 2 3 5 5 = 45 = 9

The table shows us that there is a *neutral accord* between a 6 birth number and a 9 name number. However, if we use the name Clem Attlee, which was employed by his family and colleagues, an improved accord emerges:

CLEM ATTLEE
3 3 5 4 1 2 2 3 5 5 = 33 = 6

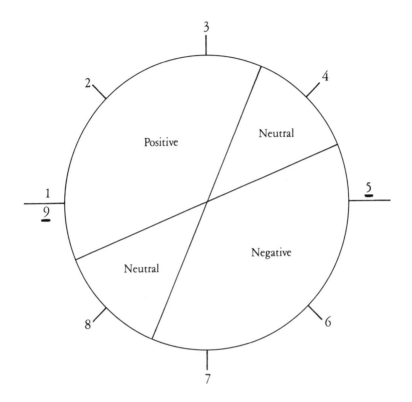

The table shows that a *positive accord* exists between a 6 birth number and a 6 name number.

The man who followed Attlee into Number 10 was Winston Churchill, who was born on 30 November 1874. His birthdate gave him a 7 birth number. His name number is 1:

WINSTON CHURCHILL
5 9 5 1 2 6 5   3 8 3 9 3 8 9 3 3 = 82 = 10 = 1

As the table shows, there is a *positive accord* between a 7 birth number and a 1 name number.

Britain's third post-war prime minister was Anthony Eden, who was born on 12 June 1897 and who thus had a 7 birth number. His name number is 8:

ANTHONY EDEN
1 5 2 8 6 5 7   5 4 5 5 = 53 = 8

Again, the table shows that there exists a *positive accord* between a birth number of 7 and a name number of 8.

The next prime minister was Harold MacMillan, who was born on 10 February 1894. This gave him a 7 birth number. His name number is 1, like Churchill's:

$$\begin{matrix} \text{H A R O L D} & \text{M A C M I L L A N} \\ \text{8 1 9 6 3 4} & \text{4 1 3 4 9 3 3 1 5} = 64 = 10 = 1 \end{matrix}$$

As we have already seen, there exists a *positive accord* between a 7 birth number and a 1 name number.

Alec Douglas-Home became Prime Minister on MacMillan's retirement in 1963. Born on 2 July 1903, he has a 4 birth number. His name number is 6:

$$\begin{matrix} \text{A L E C} & \text{D O U G L A S} - \text{H O M E} \\ \text{1 3 5 3} & \text{4 6 3 7 3 1 1} & \text{8 6 4 5} = 60 = 6 \end{matrix}$$

From the table we can see that there exists a *positive accord* between a 4 birth number and a 6 name number.

The next prime minister was Harold Wilson, who held office twice, the first time from 1964 to 1970, the second from 1974 to 1976. Born on 11 March 1916, he has a 4 birth number. His name number is 6:

$$\begin{matrix} \text{H A R O L D} & \text{W I L S O N} \\ \text{8 1 9 6 3 4} & \text{5 9 3 1 6 5} = 60 = 6 \end{matrix}$$

With the same birth number and name number as Alec Douglas-Home, Harold Wilson thus enjoys a *positive accord* between them.

Edward Heath was Prime Minister between the two tenures of Harold Wilson. He was born on 9 July 1916 and therefore has a 6 birth number. His name number is 7:

$$\begin{matrix} \text{E D W A R D} & \text{H E A T H} \\ \text{5 4 5 1 9 4} & \text{8 5 1 2 8} = 52 = 7 \end{matrix}$$

And once again, the table shows that there exists a *positive accord* between a 6 birth number and a 7 name number.

After Harold Wilson's retirement in 1976 James Callaghan became Prime Minister. Callaghan was born on 27 March 1912, a date which gives him a 7 birth number. His name number is 8:

$$\begin{matrix} \text{J A M E S} & \text{C A L L A G H A N} \\ \text{1 1 4 5 1} & \text{3 1 3 3 1 7 8 1 5} = 44 = 8 \end{matrix}$$

The table shows that there is a *positive accord* between a 7 birth number and an 8 name number.

Finally, Margaret Thatcher has been Prime Minister of Britain since 1979. Born on 13 October 1925, she has a 4 birth number. Her name number is also 4:

MARGARET   THATCHER
4 1 9 7 1 9 5 2   2 8 1 2 3 8 5 9 = 76 = 13 = 4

Because Mrs Thatcher's birth number and name number are the same, there is a *positive accord* between them.

Thus perhaps not surprisingly, each of these democratically elected British leaders, who were and are successful in both their public and private lives, have a positive accord between their birth number and their name number. Indeed, we find the same accord between the birth and name numbers of most post-war American presidents. Consider, for example, Ronald Reagan, who was a successful film actor before he turned to politics. Born on 6 February 1911, he has a 2 birth number. His name number is also 2:

RONALD   REAGAN
9 6 5 1 3 4   9 5 1 7 1 5 = 56 = 11 = 2

With the same birth number and name number, Ronald Reagan enjoys a *positive accord* between them.

James Earl Carter was the full name of the man who occupied the White House before Ronald Reagan, but he was known to all as Jimmy Carter. Born on 1 October 1924, he has a 9 birth number. His name number is likewise 9:

JIMMY   CARTER
1 9 4 4 7   3 1 9 2 5 9 = 54 = 9

This means that there exists a *positive accord* between his birth number and his name number.

The President before Jimmy Carter was Gerald Ford, who was born on 14 July 1913. This birthday gave him an 8 birth number. His name number is 9:

GERALD   FORD
7 5 9 1 3 4   6 6 9 4 = 54 = 9

Again, the table shows that there is a *positive accord* between an 8 birth number and a 9 name number.

But we do not find such a happy accord between the birth number and the name number of the White House's previous occupant, Richard Nixon, who was impeached in 1974. Nixon was born on 9 January 1913, which gave him a 6 birth number. His name number, however, is 2:

$$\begin{array}{cc} \text{R I C H A R D} & \text{N I X O N} \\ 9\ 9\ 3\ 8\ 1\ 9\ 4 & 5\ 9\ 6\ 6\ 5 = 74 = 11 = 2 \end{array}$$

The table shows that there is a *negative accord* between a 6 birth number and a 2 name number. Such an accord clearly represents, not Richard Nixon's political success, which was considerable, but his paranoia, his unhappy personal relationships, and his disgrace.

A negative accord is frequently found between the birth number and the name number of those who are tyrants and dictators, whose regimes are based on fear and oppression. These people invariably have unhappy and chaotic inner lives.

Let us take Adolf Hitler and Benito Mussolini as examples.

Adolf Hitler, who was born on 20 April 1889, had a 5 birth number. His name number is 2:

$$\begin{array}{cc} \text{A D O L F} & \text{H I T L E R} \\ 1\ 4\ 6\ 3\ 6 & 8\ 9\ 2\ 3\ 5\ 9 = 56 = 11 = 2 \end{array}$$

The table shows that there is a *negative accord* between a 5 birth number and a 2 name number.

Benito Mussolini, the Italian Fascist leader, was born on 4 December 1892, a date which gave him a 2 birth number. His name number is 7:

$$\begin{array}{cc} \text{B E N I T O} & \text{M U S S O L I N I} \\ 2\ 5\ 5\ 9\ 2\ 6 & 4\ 3\ 1\ 1\ 6\ 3\ 9\ 5\ 9 = 70 = 7 \end{array}$$

Again, the table reveals that there is a *negative accord* between a 2 birth number and a 7 name number.

Tragedy and unhappiness were frequent visitors to the life of Isadora Duncan, the dancer, who lost her two children in a boating accident, her husband through suicide and her own life when her scarf became entangled in a wheel of the car in which she was a passenger. Miss Duncan was born on 27 May 1878 and so had a 2 birth number. Her name number is 7:

$$\begin{array}{cc} \text{I S A D O R A} & \text{D U N C A N} \\ 9\ 1\ 1\ 4\ 6\ 9\ 1 & 4\ 3\ 5\ 3\ 1\ 5 = 52 = 7 \end{array}$$

With the same birth number and name number as Benito Mussolini, Isadora Duncan's life was marred by the *negative accord* that exists between them.

These examples amply demonstrate that there is a close

YOUR NUMBER ACCORD   105

relationship between the birth number/name number accord and the quality of one's life. However, because this relationship exists, it naturally offers a way of improving one's lot by the simple and relatively painless method of changing one's name. If such a change improves the accord between one's birth number and name number, then it will automatically better one's chances of happiness. This, of course, introduces a new factor into the name changes discussed in Chapter 3, which looked at the name from an internal vowel number/consonant number point of view. Inner harmony between one's ego and id does form the foundation of happiness, yet the delicate and precious edifice that can be built on it can only withstand the gales of life if it is protected by an encircling positive accord between the birth number and the name number. But all too often, people – actors and entertainers for example – change their names without realizing the hidden numerological damage they are doing to themselves.

For example, singer and film star Judy Garland was born Frances Gumm on 10 June 1922. Her 3 birth number had a *positive accord* with the name number of her proper name, which is also 3:

$$\begin{array}{ll} \text{F R A N C E S} & \text{G U M M} \\ \text{6 9 1 5 3 5 1} & \text{7 3 4 4} = 48 = 12 = 3 \end{array}$$

Such an accord promises a happy life and this promise was made brighter in Miss Gumm's case by the harmony that existed between her 9 vowel number and her 3 consonant number:

$$\begin{array}{ll} \text{F R A N C E S} & \text{G U M M} \\ \quad 1 \qquad 5 & \quad 3 \qquad = 9 \end{array}$$

$$\begin{array}{ll} \text{F R A N C E S} & \text{G U M M} \\ \text{6 9 \ 5 3 \ 1} & \text{7 \ 4 4} = 39 = 12 = 3 \end{array}$$

With such a combination Judy Garland, had she remained as Frances Gumm, would have become a lively, energetic woman, one quite capable of facing life on its own terms and with very few doubts about herself as a person. She would have had a rising spirit, a brash sense of fun and the ability to cope with her problems without resorting to drink or drugs, as indeed Judy Garland was able to before her name change. Thus she would have been, as Frances Gumm, a happy and a stable woman.

By becoming Judy Garland Frances Gumm found stardom yet stumbled into an unhappy bramble bush of marital difficulties, weight problems and a dependence on drugs which undermined her health. She once asked, 'If I'm such a legend, then why am I so lonely?' So why did this happen? Simply because she chose the wrong stage name. Judy Garland's name number is 9 which has, as the table shows, a *negative accord* with her 3 birth number:

$$\begin{array}{ll} \text{J U D Y} & \text{G A R L A N D} \\ 1\ 3\ 4\ 7 & 7\ 1\ 9\ 3\ 1\ 5\ 4 = 45 = 9 \end{array}$$

Such an accord was able to cause the damage it did to Judy Garland because her name had no inner stability. Her 5 vowel number was out of harmony with her 4 consonant number, suggesting that there were disruptive tensions between her ego and id. Thus her new name gave nothing on which she could build happiness.

$$\begin{array}{ll} \text{J U D Y} & \text{G A R L A N D} \\ \quad 3 & \quad 1 \quad\ \ 1 \quad\quad = 5 \end{array}$$

$$\begin{array}{ll} \text{J U D Y} & \text{G A R L A N D} \\ 1\ \ 4\ 7 & 7\ \ 9\ 3\ \ \ 5\ 4 = 40 = 4 \end{array}$$

Bob Dylan made a similar, yet not quite so drastic mistake. He was born Robert Zimmerman on 24 May 1941, which gave him a 7 birth number. His proper name number is 1:

$$\begin{array}{ll} \text{R O B E R T} & \text{Z I M M E R M A N} \\ 9\ 6\ 2\ 5\ 9\ 2 & 8\ 9\ 4\ 4\ 5\ 9\ 4\ 1\ 5 = 82 = 10 = 1 \end{array}$$

As the table shows, a 7 birth number and a 1 name number enjoy a *positive accord*. Equally important, the vowel number (8) and the consonant number (2) of the name Robert Zimmerman are compatible:

$$\begin{array}{ll} \text{R O B E R T} & \text{Z I M M E R M A N} \\ \ 6\ \ \ 5 & \quad 9 \quad\ \ 5 \quad\ \ 1 \quad = 26 = 8 \end{array}$$

$$\begin{array}{ll} \text{R O B E R T} & \text{Z I M M E R M A N} \\ 9\ \ 2\ \ 9\ 2 & 8\ \ 4\ 4\ \ \ 9\ 4\ \ \ 5 = 56 = 11 = 2 \end{array}$$

With these number combinations Robert Zimmerman would have grown into a well-rounded, happy man. He might not, of course, have found the fame and fortune of Bob Dylan, but his personal gains would have been just as great.

By becoming Bob Dylan, Robert Zimmermann cast a shadow over his life, for the name number of Bob Dylan is 3, which has a *negative accord* with his 7 birth number.

$$\begin{array}{ll} \text{B O B} & \text{D Y L A N} \\ 2\ 6\ 2 & 4\ 7\ 3\ 1\ 5 = 30 = 3 \end{array}$$

Such an accord means that Bob Dylan cannot be as happy as he would have been as Robert Zimmerman. However, he is protected from the worst effects of this accord by the compatible vowel number (7) and consonant number (5) of his new name:

$$\begin{array}{ccc} \text{B O B} & \text{D Y L A N} & \\ 6 & 1 & = 7 \end{array}$$

$$\begin{array}{ccc} \text{B O B} & \text{D Y L A N} & \\ 2\ \ 2 & 4\ 7\ 3\ \ \ 5 & = 23 = 5 \end{array}$$

Because a 7 ego and a 5 id are compatible, they give Bob Dylan sufficient inner stability to withstand the difficulties that life throws at him, so that while he will never be really happy he won't go under either. And because 7 and 5 symbolize strong creative talents and an adventurous spirit, they represent the bedrock on which Bob Dylan built his success as a singer and composer.

This naturally brings us again to you and your life. Like everyone else, you want to be happy. You want to wake up in the morning with a song in your heart, secure in the knowledge that others like you because you are nice to know. You might already feel like this. If so, you are blessed indeed, loved by the gods. If not, then it is time you examined your name numbers and made any name change that might be necessary.

But first, find out the accord that exists between your birth number and your name number. If this is positive, next check which life period you are in. You may be living through a single negative period or a double negative period. These always bring problems of one sort or another, even to those whose birth number and name number are in positive accord. If this is the case, then you should see how compatible your vowel number and consonant number are. Should these be incompatible you can improve your inner strength by changing your name to make them compatible. However, you must make sure that your name number maintains a positive accord with your birth number. Of course, if your birth number has a negative or neutral accord with your name number, you should certainly change your name to produce a positive accord. This is particularly important if you happen to be living through a single negative period or a double negative period.

To make this quite clear, let us consider the case of Rosemary Brown and the disruptive effect that marriage had on her name – and the simple remedy she found for it. Since she was a schoolgirl

Rosemary Brown had called herself Rose Brown and she was a happy, well-adjusted girl. Born on 11 March 1960, she has a 3 birth number. Her name number is also 3:

$$\text{R O S E} \quad \text{B R O W N}$$
$$9\ 6\ 1\ 5 \quad 2\ 9\ 6\ 5\ 5 = 48 = 12 = 3$$

The table shows that between a 3 birth number and a 3 name number there is a *positive accord*. This favourable accord was backed up by a compatible vowel number (8) and consonant number (4):

$$\text{R O S E} \quad \text{B R O W N}$$
$$6 \quad 5 \qquad 6 \qquad = 17 = 8$$

$$\text{R O S E} \quad \text{B R O W N}$$
$$9 \quad 1 \qquad 2\ 9 \quad 5\ 5 = 31 = 4$$

When Rose met handsome George Smith and they fell in love, her happiness seemed assured. But when they married shortly after her 22nd birthday things couldn't have gone more wrong. They had trouble in finding somewhere to live and Rose, quite unaccountably, became depressed, irritable and unhappy. And after an argument with her employer she left her job, which made the Smiths short of money. Things steadily worsened. It soon began to look as though the marriage would not last.

The answer lay, as we might expect, in the name change that Rose had undergone when she married. From Rose Brown she had become Rose Smith, and Rose Smith not only gave her a different name number (9) but a different vowel number (2) and consonant number (7) as well:

$$\text{R O S E} \quad \text{S M I T H}$$
$$9\ 6\ 1\ 5 \quad 1\ 4\ 9\ 2\ 8 = 45 = 9$$

The table shows that between Rose's 3 birth number and her new name number there is a *negative accord*. This accord was made worse by the fact that she was then living through the last year of a double negative life period, whose damaging potential it unleashed.

The name change also gave her an incompatible ego and id, which explains why she became a different person so quickly. For Rose Brown wanted so much to be Mrs Rose Smith.

$$\text{R O S E} \quad \text{S M I T H}$$
$$6 \quad 5 \qquad 9 \qquad = 20 = 2$$

$$\text{R O S E} \quad \text{S M I T H}$$
$$9 \quad 1 \qquad 1\ 4 \quad 2\ 8 = 25 = 7$$

But fortunately, Rose Smith found her own salvation. Quite instinctively, she began calling herself Rosemary Smith, perhaps feeling that Rosemary Smith had more natural dignity than Rose Smith. It was a change that brought her out of her depression and saved her marriage. Indeed, she is now the happy, smiling young woman you would wish her to be. And a bird recently whispered that a Smith Junior is on the way!

The change to Rosemary Smith gave her back her original name number:

R O S E M A R Y   S M I T H
9 6 1 5 4 1 9 7   1 4 9 2 8 = 66 = 12 = 3

It also gave her a compatible vowel number (3) and consonant number (9):

R O S E M A R Y   S M I T H
  6   5   1   9   = 21 = 3

R O S E M A R Y   S M I T H
9   1   4   9 7   1 4   2 8 = 45 = 9

If you believe that a name change can improve your life, you might be able to make the change as easily as Rosemary Smith or Peter Jones did. But it is quite probable that you might have to adopt a completely new Christian name to bring about the number changes that you desire. In this respect it is pertinent to note that there is no law against you changing your name, so long as this is not done with intent to defraud. However, a radical name change is inconvenient, especially where official documents are concerned.

But while inconvenient in a public and private sense, such a change will bring you positive personal benefits. Within a short time you will find your mood and your confidence changing for the better, and in the wake of these changes will come improvements in your relationships and circumstances that will upgrade the whole quality of your life. For no matter what sort of life period you are now in you can make things better for yourself with a careful name change.

So don't delay. Get the right numbers working for you with a new name. They will change your life more significantly and more positively than a big win on the pools or in a lottery.

For they will give you the greatest blessing of all: happiness.

Index